Cambridge Elements ☰

Elements in Pragmatics
edited by
Jonathan Culpeper
Lancaster University, UK
Michael Haugh
University of Queensland, Australia

PRAGMATICS IN TRANSLATION

Mediality, Participation and Relational Work

Daria Dayter
Tampere University

Miriam A. Locher
University of Basel

Thomas C. Messerli
University of Basel

CAMBRIDGE
UNIVERSITY PRESS

Shaftesbury Road, Cambridge CB2 8EA, United Kingdom

One Liberty Plaza, 20th Floor, New York, NY 10006, USA

477 Williamstown Road, Port Melbourne, VIC 3207, Australia

314–321, 3rd Floor, Plot 3, Splendor Forum, Jasola District Centre, New Delhi – 110025, India

103 Penang Road, #05–06/07, Visioncrest Commercial, Singapore 238467

Cambridge University Press is part of Cambridge University Press & Assessment, a department of the University of Cambridge.

We share the University's mission to contribute to society through the pursuit of education, learning and research at the highest international levels of excellence.

www.cambridge.org
Information on this title: www.cambridge.org/9781009261203

DOI: 10.1017/9781009261210

Published with the support of the Swiss National Science Foundation.

First published 2023

A catalogue record for this publication is available from the British Library.

ISBN 978-1-009-26120-3 Paperback
ISSN 2633-6464 (online)
ISSN 2633-6456 (print)

Pragmatics in Translation

Mediality, Participation and Relational Work

Elements in Pragmatics

DOI: 10.1017/9781009261210
First published online: January 2023

Daria Dayter
Tampere University

Miriam A. Locher
University of Basel

Thomas C. Messerli
University of Basel

Author for correspondence: Daria Dayter, daria.dayter@tuni.fi

Abstract: This Element addresses translation within an interpersonal pragmatics frame. The aims of this Element are twofold: first, the authors survey the current state of the field of pragmatics in translation; second, they present the current and methodologically innovative avenues of research in the field. They focus on three pragmatics issues – mediality, participation structure and relational work – that they foreground as promising loci of research on translational data. By reviewing the trajectory of pragmatics research on translation/interpreting over time and then outlining their understanding of pragmatics in translation as a field, they arrive at a set of potential research questions which represent desiderata for future research. These questions identify the paths that can be productively explored through synergies between the linguistic pragmatics framework and translation data. In two case study sections, the authors offer two example studies addressing some of the questions identified as suggestions for future research. This title is also available as Open Access on Cambridge Core.

Keywords: relational work, interpersonal pragmatics, pragmatics in translation, audiovisual translation, simultaneous interpreting

ISBNs: 9781009261203 (PB), 9781009261210 (OC)
ISSNs: 2633-6464 (online), 2633-6456 (print)

Contents

1 Introduction   1

2 Translation through the Pragmatic Lens   7

3 Interpreting through the Pragmatic Lens   14

4 Audiovisual translation through the Pragmatic Lens   22

5 Conveying Risky Intent in Simultaneous Interpreting   29

6 Relational Work in Korean Drama Subtitling and Live
  Comments   42

7 Where Next?   56

  References   66

1 Introduction

1.1 Translation – Narrow and Wide Definitions

What happens to the pragmatic level of language – the meaning of words dependent on their context and the interlocutors' shared background knowledge – in translation? An example can be found in an anecdote about intercultural communication. The story goes that when former US President Jimmy Carter was giving a speech at a Methodist college in Japan, he began with a joke. After the interpreter's utterance, the audience broke into incredible laughter. In a conversation afterwards, the interpreter admitted that he had said, 'Mr. Carter just told a funny story. Everyone must laugh like crazy' (Moore, 2013: 60). Although one may doubt the veracity of this particular story, one of the authors of this Element can testify that this is an interpreting technique explicitly taught to interpreting students during their training. In pragmatic terms, it can be rendered as follows: if you cannot translate the illocution, translate the perlocution. The anecdote illustrates that translating pragmatic phenomena is not always straightforward and merits linguistic study to describe the transformations and shifts such phenomena undergo in different media and participant constellations.

This Element addresses translation issues within an interpersonal pragmatics frame and maps out potential research questions that arise within that frame and with regard to novel types of data. We envision the Element as a research guide for scholars interested in applying contemporary pragmatic theory to translational data. To achieve this aim, we combine state-of-the-art overviews of existing research with concrete suggestions of unexplored research questions and suitable data types to answer these questions. Two case studies offer detailed examples of interpersonal pragmatics research into non-prototypical data types: simultaneous interpreting in high-stakes political contexts and fan subtitling of Korean drama.

These two examples appear to be very different from each other, and yet they both constitute translational data. Before tackling the subject of pragmatics in translation, it is important to define what we understand under 'translation'. Although the first, most salient definition of 'translation' to come to a reader's mind is probably concerned with an activity of establishing some form of equivalence between two written texts – one source, one target – in this Element we approach translation from a more inclusive perspective. We include under the heading of 'translation' a host of related activities, such as written translation and oral simultaneous and consecutive interpreting carried out by professionals and community interpreters alike, but also localisation, fan translation, audiovisual translation and subtitling, signing (intermodal translation), explaining meaning to each other, and even rendering sensual experience into language.

The issue of the discipline label and terminology has long occupied the minds of translation studies scholars (see, for example, Holmes' classic 'The name and nature of translation studies' ([1972] 2000), or Chesterman et al.'s tongue-in-cheek 'Bananas: On names and definitions in translation studies' (2003)). This is not an argument this Element intends to revisit. As linguists, our interest lies primarily in the descriptive approach to language varieties involved in translation and how the tools of linguistic pragmatics may help shed light on those varieties.

In this section of the Element, we first clarify the scope of pragmatics in translation. We then identify the three key analytical issues that will appear in every subsequent section. The section is concluded with the outline of the Element structure, which points out the target audience for each section.

1.2 Pragmatics in Translation

The concern with pragmatics is naturally not new to the study of translation: it goes as far back as Nida's (1964) work discussing pragmatic equivalence in Bible translations. Linguists have also brought classic pragmatic concepts such as politeness, relevance, deixis and presupposition to the study of translated text (Hickey, 1998). We do not offer an extensive review of this work in our Element, as this is a task that is not achievable in this short format and that is already fulfilled by other excellent contributions on the topic, for example, Tipton and Desilla (2019).

However, in order to make clear our aims and the scope of the Element, we would like to draw the reader's attention to the title of this last publication. Tipton and Desilla (2019) chose to name their edited volume *The Routledge Handbook of Translation and Pragmatics,* placing translation and pragmatics on equal footing by means of the coordinating conjunction 'and'. Other sub-disciplines dealing with related topics of pragmatic phenomena across linguistic cultures bear the names of cross-cultural pragmatics (see House & Kádár, 2021), intercultural pragmatics (see Kecskés, 2013) or contrastive pragmatics (see Aijmer, 2011) and have their own developed tradition and canon. They focus on the study of language use across 'linguacultures' (Friedrich, 1989), the communicative processes among people from different cultures speaking different L1s, and the contrastive study of pragmatics in different languages to inform teaching, respectively.

By choosing to talk instead about pragmatics in translation, we want to foreground our primary concern with translation outcomes and processes that highlight the pragmatic angle of understanding the transfer of language phenomena across cultures and intraculturally. Therefore, our interest lies in addressing questions about what happens to pragmatic phenomena when they are being translated. Our aim is to identify the contemporary pragmatic theories and angles that deserve more attention in the study of translated language, and to suggest a range of promising research questions to guide future research and fill those gaps. Rather than positioning ourselves in contrast to disciplines such as contrastive pragmatics or translation studies, we argue that pragmatics in translation can draw on existing research findings, while shifting the focus from a central interest in translation to a central interest in pragmatics.

We believe that especially interpersonal pragmatics and relational work can inform future research in this area. They constitute the contemporary take on the issues related to politeness that have hitherto been analysed through politeness frameworks that focus on the speaker's possibilities to minimise face-threat (e.g. Brown & Levinson, 1987). Interpersonal pragmatics and relational work theories argue that linguistic resources acquire their meaning in context through negotiation of societal norms (Locher & Graham, 2010). They provide improved descriptive adequacy that reflects the fluid nature of human communication. The focus on relational work is reflected in the structure of each section, which includes a discussion of this approach in the translational data type under scrutiny.

We also aim to ask questions about novel types of translational data that are currently under-researched in pragmatics-centred work. Two of these – simultaneous interpreting in high-stakes political contexts, and translation of culture in Korean drama fan subtitles and viewer comments – are illustrated in the case studies in Sections 5 and 6. In Section 7, we offer open-ended questions about further data types, such as automatically translated social media posts and captions, remote interpreting, community interpreting and translation apps. We hope that the Element will help pave the way to exciting new research and encourage young scholars to tackle the research questions posed in Section 7.

1.3 Key Issues

Throughout this Element, we focus on three key issues that play an important role in our understanding of the research direction to be taken in pragmatics in translation. These issues are not on the same level of generality: two can be broadly identified as theoretical approaches to analysing communication, and the third is a characteristic of the data. However, these issues resurface again and again in our discussions of how linguistic pragmatics can inform the investigation of novel translational data. Below, we introduce and define these issues. They will be highlighted in every one of the following five sections, although the amount of attention given to each will shift depending on the focus of the section.

- Mediality

  The concept of mediality, borrowed from media studies (see Papacharissi, 2015), is a useful tool for the discussion at hand. Complementing modality, which refers to individual modes such as text or image, mediality foregrounds the multimodal contexts and interweaving of different media (for example, when interpreters rely both on printed text and live speech as input). Mediality also captures the influence that the material medium has on the linguistic one, describing e.g. how the simultaneous orality of conference interpreting shapes the linguistic output. Incorporating a wider variety of activities into the scope of 'translation' in this Element means that the medium, or modality, in which the translation is accomplished comes to the forefront of analytical considerations. While the translation 'prototype' is written text to written text, we are going to have to take into account other mode constellations. Interpreting involves oral-to-oral rendering, sometimes accompanied by written to oral (sight translation, or reading a document out loud in the target language). Another possible intermodal constellation is oral to gesture (sign interpreting). There are also translation types that involve more than one parallel process: for example, translating a film may involve translating a script to be spoken by the dubbing actors and translating subtitles, with these two not necessarily working with the same source (the subtitler might be working from the closed captions in the source language, for example, which are already adapted in length). Simultaneous interpreting with text is another complex process, involving sight translation supplemented by genuine simultaneous interpreting to incorporate any ad hoc changes the speaker may make to the prepared speech. Even less prototypical types of intermodal translation are, for instance, visual to spoken, as in audio descriptions of films for the visually impaired, or 'sensual to written' translation, which happens when a professional food taster describes taste. Although mediality is often taken for granted in pragmatics studies of translation, we will explicitly address this aspect of the data in every section as it may have crucial influence on the pragmatics phenomena under discussion.

- Participation framework

  Goffman (1981) introduced the terms 'participation status', 'footing' and 'participation framework' to differentiate how people involved in an inter-actional setting participate in that setting: as addressees, speakers, bystanders, overhearers etc. This approach was soon adopted in linguistics in order to go beyond the confines of the 'traditional [. . .] threefold division between speaker, hearer, and something spoken about' (Hymes, 1972: 58). A nuanced differentiation among participant roles enabled analysts to be more precise about participants' alignment and orientation to the talk in progress. Describing the participation status for understanding pragmatic phenomena becomes especially important in translation and interpreting contexts, where participants' constellations are complex and sometimes partly hidden.

- Relational work
  Relational work is a concept pertaining to interpersonal pragmatics, i.e. the study of the interpersonal side of language in use. Relational work is the linguistic and multimodal '"work" individuals invest in negotiating relationships with others' (Locher & Watts, 2005: 10), and interpersonal pragmatics approaches argue that linguistic resources used to realise relational work acquire their meaning in context through negotiation of societal norms. The study of (im)politeness phenomena is subsumed within relational work. Accepting that linguistic (im)politeness is fundamentally context-dependent has far-reaching implications for the study of (im)politeness in translation and interpreting due to the shift of context from production to reception as well as different background knowledge of the intended vs. factual audience. In addition, relational work and identity construction are interlinked, since how a speaker chooses language reflects their knowledge about (im)politeness norms and they are being assessed against these norms. Locher and Sidiropoulou (2021) therefore identify 'identity construction and relational work' as one of the challenges for translation that warrants being explored further. Sidiropoulou (2021) is a recent example of tackling this challenge with regard to written translation.

1.4 Structure of the Element

The Element consists of seven sections. Although we tried to create a sense of trajectory throughout the sections, unfolding the narrative from some background on pragmatics in translation towards a few specific examples and then a glance into the future, the sections can also be read in isolation. Below we will outline the content of each section and conclude with hints on when the section might come in as especially helpful.

- Section 2 provides a bird's-eye view of the research to date on written translational data, highlighting the development of linguistic pragmatic theories brought to bear on this data. This section sets the stage for the remainder of the Element by contextualising the three key themes – mediality, participation framework and relational work – in translation.

- ◦ Read this section if you are new to the field and are looking to get your bearings before starting a research project on pragmatics of translational data.

- Section 3 surveys pragmatic research on data from consecutive, liaison and whisper, and simultaneous interpreting. We highlight the prominence and productivity of some models and compare this output to other, more recent, pragmatic theories.

  - ◦ Read this section if you would like to familiarise yourself with the main pragmatic issues in interpreting and to find out what has been done in interpreting research from the relational work perspective.

- Section 4 highlights specific aspects of audiovisual translation (AVT) as situated language use. AVT comprises activities like dubbing (voice-to-voice), which are arguably in some ways closer to interpreting than to text-to-text translation, and subtitling (retained voice, translated into additional written text).

  - ◦ Read this section if you are interested in film and TV translation in dubbed and subtitled form.

- Section 5 adopts the relational work framework and presents a case study of conference interpreters' treatment of the interpersonal pragmatic phenomena in high-stakes political discourse.

  - ◦ Read this section if you need help designing a research project that uses a corpus to investigate politeness phenomena in interpreting.

- Section 6 showcases Locher and Messerli's work on identifying cross-culturally salient moments of relational work as made accessible in the translations of lay subtitlers and in the comments by online viewers of these scenes.

  - ◦ Read this section if you need help designing a research project that works with fictional data and involves heterogeneous groups that engage with the artefact in complex sense-making processes.

- Section 7 highlights the areas of research that can offer the most productive synergies between contemporary pragmatic theories and the unique product- and process-oriented data that translation and interpreting provide. We conclude with a set of research questions that address these gaps and directions for further research.

  - ◦ Read this section if you are looking for inspiration to build a research project on pragmatics in translation.

2 Translation through the Pragmatic Lens

2.1 Introduction

In this section, we limit our scope through the factor of mediality: we explore translation in the narrower sense, i.e. rendering a written text in one language into written text in another. While this concept of translation is easier to delimit than the broad understanding we have offered in Section 1, its definition is not straightforward. The necessary conditions just mentioned are of course not sufficient, since translators and readers of translated texts also have particular expectations regarding the relationship between source and target texts. Outside of scholarly and professional discourses, a lay understanding of translation may well be captured in a circular fashion: a translated text is the product of translation – translation produces translated texts. But attempting a non-circular definition that can properly define the relationship between original and translated texts is a more difficult endeavour. House (2018b: 9), for instance, defines translation as the replacement of one text by another in a different language. This is accurate unless we focus on texts where original and translation are side by side and the target text is thus an addition rather than a replacement (e.g. bilingual editions of books), but leaves open what kind of replacing text counts as a translation. House (2019: 10) herself, while not including any further aspects in the definition, goes on to add further attributes such as translation being secondary communication, a type of repetition, in a relationship of semantic and pragmatic equivalence with the source text and in a *double-bind relationship* with source text and target context.

Pragmatics is often described along the lines of two traditions. The first is the Anglo-American one, closely related to philosophy of language and preoccupied with theorising implicature and presupposition, speech acts, deixis, etc. The second is the European tradition, which takes a broad view of what communicating meaning in context entails, and also includes the study of language in use from a social and cultural vantage point. In translation studies, the interest has slowly shifted from the Anglo-American view to the broader Continental-European approach. We adopt the same broader view of pragmatics here and are interested in translation as situated language use including explicit as well as implicit meaning. Due to the complex textual, contextual and intertextual relationships that characterise translations, they are rich sources for the exploration of pragmatic meaning, and we will shed light on some of the most relevant aspects in this and the subsequent two sections. Section 2.2 will highlight some avenues of pragmatic research in translation that have been pursued. Section 2.3 will outline the participation frameworks in which translation is situated. Section 2.4 focuses on aspects of relational work in translation in particular. The bird's-eye view we offer in this section, summarised in Section 2.5, will then be complemented with more detailed accounts of interpreting studies in Section 3 and audiovisual translation in Section 4.

2.2 Translation and Research in Pragmatics

To understand what research has been done in the pragmatics in or of translation, it is useful to acknowledge that, historically, translation studies have had little interest in pragmatics and that pragmatics, similarly, has not regarded translation as a type of situated language use that needs to be studied. From a core pragmatic perspective, to this day often informed by introspective examples of typical language use, translation is perhaps too peripheral and too far removed from a basic language setting to have garnered much interest (a view we do not share). Translation studies, on the other hand, has developed surprisingly independently of linguistic scholarship and has only recently begun to incorporate macroscopic views of context and settings as research foci.

Although the work by, e.g., the Leipzig school of translation scholars included mentions of 'pragmatics', the term did not have the scope it has today. Kade (1968) referred to 'pragmatic texts' as one type of source texts, namely, the ones where form is subordinated to content (in contrast to 'literary texts'). Neubert (1968) further differentiated among literary-type and pragmatic-type texts based on the idea of communicative equivalence. Similarly, Jäger (1975) narrowly focused on 'functional' versus 'communicative' equivalence. The relevant influential work directly starts from speech act theory to theorise the cultural specificity not only of particular speech acts but also of the felicity conditions in different cultural contexts. Blum-Kulka (1981) establishes that the translatability of indirect speech acts depends on whether the relevant felicity conditions are universal or culture-specific, whereas Blum-Kulka and Olshtain (1984) attempt to find pragmatic universals (not to be confused with the translation studies-specific concept of 'translation universals') based on the example of requests and apologies in different translations. A seminal contribution in translation studies is Hatim and Mason (1997), who, building on the work by Nida (1964), House (1977) and other scholars with an interest in functional equivalence, specifically positioned translation as communication. Rather than adhering to the tradition of focusing on specific aspects of translation practices that differ based on the text type they translate and produce, Hatim and Mason (1997) attempt a more general conceptualisation of the work of translators, who essentially need skills to process text in the source language, skills to transfer it and productive skills in the target language. The difference between formal and functional aspects of source and target texts had already been discussed by Nida (1964) in terms of formal and dynamic equivalence, and Hatim and Mason (1997) further take inspiration from Bell's (1984) notion of audience design (see also Mason, 2000; House, 2018b: 54–5) to arrive at their understanding of translation as a communicative practice. The translator as communicator is first a reader, who takes into account the sociocultural context of the source text to identify presuppositions and implicatures and arrive at a coherent understanding of what the text means, before communicating it in the target language by transferring and producing it in a manner pertinent to the sociocultural context in which the target text will be situated.

Another key aspect in the development of a pragmatics of translation and translated text is the systematic inclusion of context, for which House's (e.g. 2006, 2015, 2018a, 2018b) work is of importance. We will approach this understanding of context and the understanding of translation as recontextualisation as relevant for the participation framework of translation and address it in Section 2.3.

Finally, Morini's (2013: 155) self-declared 'little Copernican revolution' in his monograph *The Pragmatic Translator* approaches translation in terms of performative, locative and interpersonal functions and with the explicit goal of bridging the gap between what he considers distant theorisations from the outside and applicable tools for the translator. While Morini's main interest appears to be a shift in focus away from the product of translation to translation as a process, a step he deems crucial for the usefulness of translation theory for practitioners, we can add to this a desideratum for studying the conceptualisation of the reception of translated texts, and thus a shift away from the translator to the reader who has entered translation studies for the most part only as a mental model of the translator when designing a target text for an audience. In other words, we need to add all contributing participants to the understanding of translation as a product and as a process.

2.3 Participation Framework

To observe translational processes and products through a pragmatic lens is to understand them as situated language use, subject to the influence not only of the translator but also of the settings in which translation takes place and translated texts are received. When looking at translation within the subdisciplines we cover in this section and in Sections 3 and 4, the crucial role of mediality is evident. The majority of work on participation, in the situation of translation in a communicative context, has been done either in interpreting studies or in AVT. In interpreting studies, it was facilitated by Wadensjö's (1998; see also Section 3) important contribution to the theorisation of participation frameworks. In AVT, Messerli (2020, 2021), for example, has offered insights into how subtitles and subtitlers position themselves and are understood as speakers in communication. Even in interpreting and AVT, no full account of meaning-making in context has been provided – and this is even more true for written translation, where only peripheral cases have been discussed specifically in terms of participants and their roles (see e.g. İkizoğlu, 2019 for a discussion of mobile phone translation apps as conversation participants).

However, insofar as participation is understood as a concretisation of context, important theorisations of the settings in which written translation takes place have been offered by Baker (1992, 2006) and House (2006), among others. Baker (2006) argues that a combination of a more cognitive (in the tradition of van Dijk, 2001) and a more social (e.g. Hymes, 1964) understanding of context is fruitful, as it makes it possible to situate the decision-making processes of both translators and recipients with regard to existing models of what translation entails, the cultural surroundings in which it takes place and the participating voices that animate it.

In contrast, House (2006) posits a translation-as-recontextualisation theory and highlights the differences in context between written and spoken interaction, which – in her opinion – render purely discursive approaches to context unfit for the conception of written translation. In a prototypical translation setting, texts are not communicated bit by bit. Instead, translators animate a static text whose context is defined and hegemonised solely by the translators rather than jointly negotiated by all participants involved. Translation in this view is thus 'an ex post facto, solitarily cognitive pragmatic process of meaning negotiation' (House, 2006: 343) over which recipients have no control. In House's view, translators navigate between and are doubly bound by the source text as a holistic entity and the target context in which their text will be understood. They strive for functional equivalence by taking into account various systems, to use the terminology of systemic functional linguistics that informs House's theory. These systems are *Genre*, *Register*, *Field*, *Mode* and *Tenor*, the latter describing the participant relationships that form part of the setting. The role of these participants in the understanding of translated texts is influenced by an understanding of the translation as overt or covert. Overt translation (e.g. of political speeches) is a process that self-identifies as translation, and is characterised by a form of recontextualisation that simultaneously activates source and target contexts (House, 2006: 356). Covert, invisible translation (e.g. of user manuals) applies a *cultural filter* in order to adapt to the target culture's communicative norms (House, 2006: 356).

A radically different take is offered by those who apply relevance theory to translation (e.g. Gutt, 1998; Gallai, 2019). Since the reading of a translated text is communication between a translator and a target audience, there is no difference in principle between translation and non-translation. As any speaker would, translators design their writing for their readers, based on assumptions they make about context in a cognitive sense, i.e. the predispositions and expectations of the target audience. The characteristics of translation, then, are to be found in the translator's decision-making regarding the meaning of the source text and its rendering in descriptive or interpretative language, and translation as a text type that shapes the aforementioned expectations towards the target text.

A promising avenue in the theorisation of written translation as communication seems to be a combination of a more specific and detailed understanding of relevant contexts or indeed participation structures, as it is outlined in the functional approaches, and the more target-audience-centred understanding that is implied by relevance theoretic approaches. Starting from the premise that the sole point of contact between writers and readers is the text, and that this point of contact is removed by translation (Malmkjaer, 1998), a pragmatic look at the participation framework of literary and other written translation may want to explore the situated communicative acts that ensue when direct contact is replaced by indirect mediation via translation.

It may be satisfactory in some traditional settings to assume that authors write texts for readers, while translators are eavesdroppers-cum-authors in the sense of Goffman (1981) (see further discussion in Section 3). Even in this conception of text translation, it is worthwhile to reflect further on the relationship between the translator as author and animator, who phrases and utters the text, and the original author as principal, who is identified explicitly (e.g. on a book cover) as the locus of values and beliefs. For instance, we may note that translators are not ratified participants in the communicative act of writing the text, but they infer the speaker's intention based on the text and perhaps in conversation with the author. To conceptualise the point of view of the readers of translated texts, we may start with their understanding of the text as a primary text or as a translation, and accordingly ask on whose behalf readers assume the written text to speak.

2.4 Relational Work

Despite the discursive turn in (im)politeness research (e.g. Locher & Watts, 2005, 2008; Spencer-Oatey, 2005a; Linguistic Politeness Research Group, 2011) that led us from the description of marked instances of face-threatening behaviour and their mitigation to a context-bound, situationally constructed understanding of interpersonal pragmatics, Brown and Levinson's (1987) politeness theory has remained influential in translation studies. Its ease of applicability means that in source and target texts, face-threatening acts (FTA) can be identified and compared in terms of their realisation, but a more general concept of the discursive construction of the relationship between writers, texts and readers eludes much of the existing scholarship.

A notable exception is the recent monograph by Sidiropoulou (2021), which incorporates the relational work perspective in its analysis of two subtypes of translation: English–Greek translations of non-fiction and of fiction. Sidiropoulou (2021) finds that in non-fictional (mass media and academic) texts, both the source writer and the translator confine themselves to the appropriate (politic) zone of the relational work scale. This finding corresponds to the research presented in Section 5 of this Element, which looks at non-fictional data as well, namely, spoken political discourse. Section 5.3 offers a more detailed review of the relational work spectrum, which the reader may wish to refer to along with this recap. With regard to fictional texts, however, Sidiropoulou (2021) establishes that the non-politic zone is the more operative one here, presumably because non-politic choices heighten emotions. The interpersonal dynamic between the text producers and receivers emerges as an important factor in the analysis, and the translator is shown to be capable of renegotiating the author's facework with the reader.

In a similar vein, Morini (2019), for instance, shows on the one hand that there is much to be gained by going beyond character-to-character pragmatics in source and target texts and complementing it with writer–reader interpersonal pragmatics. On the other hand, he attributes the same absolute notion of impoliteness to the communication between Celenza's Italian translation and Virginia Woolf's source text *To the Lighthouse* and their respective readerships. By applying Grice's maxims to source and target text and working with the idea of making implicit meaning explicit, he comes to the conclusion that Woolf is more impolite to her readers as her style employs 'free indirect thought and a conversational style [that is] used to blur the conventional divide between narrator and characters' (Morini, 2019: 195). In contrast, Celenza's translation, which employs explicitation and disambiguation, is argued to better accommodate the need of the readers for easier accessibility and therefore to be more polite (Morini, 2019: 196). These comments are made as if there were universal norms that regulate the interpersonal relationships between authors and readers and as if these norms were identical for translator–reader communication.[1]

---

[1] Later in the chapter, Morini (2019: 199) modifies his universalist stance by mentioning that the interpretation of implicatures in Jane Austen's *Pride and Prejudice* depends on the knowledge of social and economic conditions of the time.

In contrast, understanding the same texts from a relational work point of view would mean that, rather than being governed by static norms, translations, just as much as novels, establish in situ what constitutes unmarked and marked (im)polite behaviour when interacting with their readers and their respective backgrounds. For instance, we may go along with Morini and assume that making it easy for the readers to understand the basic narrative of a text may be a more polite option for the author. And in contrast, requiring much processing in order to arrive at an understanding of the events that are taking place may be less polite. Crucially, though, these norms of readability are themselves dependent on sociohistorical context, among other things (see Sidiropoulou, 2021: 9 on this point; Morini, 2019: 199 for a discussion of a passage from Jane Austen). Pollali and Sidiropoulou (2021), for example, show how different Greek translations of Eugene O'Neill's playtext *Desire under the Elms* (1924) demonstrate different orientations by the translators to expectations and ideologies prevailing in the Greek target culture in 1947 and 2017.

In addition, translations are not only governed by norms of readability but also by translation norms (Toury, 1995; Morini, 2019) that shape the relationship of the target text's reading experience with that of the source text. Establishing such translator–reader politeness norms as they are constructed in individual texts, idiosyncratically by translators or sociohistorically at different points in time, is a fascinating research area that as of yet remains underexplored.

More generally, testimony to the fact that a broadening of politeness research in translation is underway is the recent appearance of a special issue on *Pragmatics of Translation* by Locher and Sidiropoulou (2021), which contains several articles that highlight the connection between relational work and identity construction in actor/ character rendition in written translation (Sidiropoulou, 2020; Kefala, 2021; Pollali & Sidiropoulou, 2021), and Sidiropoulou's (2021) *Understanding Im/politeness through Translation*, which discusses the role of the translator with respect to (im)politeness considerations in several types of written translation from a relational work perspective. At the time of writing, however, published (im)politeness-oriented research in translation is dominated largely by comparisons of isolated instances of (im)politeness. In this area, Aijmer's (e.g. 2011) work in contrastive pragmatics as well as Hatim's (1998) application of Brown and Levinson's theory to texts are notable forward-thinking theorisations that pave the way for a truly discursive understanding of interpersonal pragmatics of translation.

2.5 Summary

Our bird's-eye view of the pragmatic aspects of the translation of texts, as well as translated texts themselves, has outlined some important areas – in particular participation frameworks and relational work – we will further pursue in Sections 3 and 4 for the cases of interpretation and AVT. Regarding participation, we have observed that the conceptualisation of written translation has not proceeded as far as that of interpreting or AVT, whereas relational work and a general situated understanding of politeness in written translation processes and products remains largely unexplored as a heuristic for the understanding of interpersonal aspects in all areas of translation.

3 Interpreting through the Pragmatic Lens

3.1 Introduction

Interpreting involves rendering speech into another language in oral modality and under time pressure; these factors of mediality and temporality converge to necessitate a separate discussion of interpreting from the viewpoint of pragmatics. Contrary to translators, interpreters have no opportunity for long deliberations, consulting dictionaries or post-editing. Another difference from translation is that interpreters are often physically co-present with the discourse participants, which plays a role in participation framework-oriented pragmatic research.

Interpreting can be subdivided into three main types along the time and participation axes: (1) consecutive/dialogue/liaison interpreting, (2) whisper interpreting and (3) conference interpreting. Much oral translation is done *consecutively*, i.e. after the source-language utterance has been uttered in full. Consecutive interpreting may be assisted by handwritten notes that the interpreter takes if the speaker's turn is very long. When working without notes and on shorter turns, consecutive interpreting is sometimes called *dialogue* or *liaison interpreting*. If only one of the participants needs interpretation to understand the proceedings, *whisper interpreting*, also called *chuchotage*, is employed, and the interpreter stands next to the client and whispers simultaneous interpretation into their ear. Finally, *conference interpreting* (essentially, simultaneous interpreting for large audiences) is performed in a special booth with interpreters working in teams of two or three, wearing headphones and speaking into a microphone at the same time as the original speech is being delivered.

Although many conceptual findings from translation studies have been applied to interpreting studies, it is a communicative activity different from written translation on so many levels as to merit a separate investigation. Just some of the key distinctions include time pressure, oral modality of reception and production, necessity to adjust the length of the target to the source speech, and tendency to work with different genres than translation. These factors contribute to a demanding environment, which is bound to have an effect on all levels of the target output, including pragmatics. In what follows, we will first introduce strands of pragmatic research in interpreting in Section 3.2 before focusing on the pragmatic research areas which are the participation framework (Section 3.3), politeness research in general (Section 3.4) and relational work in particular (Section 3.5).

3.2 Strands of Pragmatic Research in Interpreting

As Baumgarten (2017: 523) notes with respect to translation, the central problem from the pragmatic perspective lies in the cross-cultural comparability of linguistic form–function relationships. Achieving such comparability of pragmatic effect in the source and the target speech has been the subject of pragmatic research in translation and interpreting studies.

To facilitate the recipient's understanding, an interpreter may need to go to extra lengths to explain dense and technical information to the client (Gibb & Good, 2014 on refugee status hearings), elicit more detailed answers (Jacobsen, 2008 on court interpreting) or interpret power moves such as intentional silences (Nakane, 2014 on police interviews). To theorise the process, researchers have drawn on pragmatic concepts such as common ground, relevance, mitigation and aggravation, deixis and politeness formulae.

A translation model that has proven fruitful for understanding interpreting in particular is Gutt's (1998) 'interpretive resemblance'. Gutt's angle on translated language can be seen as a very early version of the more recent approaches (such as Kruger & van Rooy, 2016) that see translated language as simply one type of secondary, constrained or 'interpretive' communication. Gutt's interpretive resemblance approach, rooted in relevance theory (Sperber & Wilson, 1995), treats an utterance as an ostensive stimulus that signals to the addressee the speaker's intention to convey relevant information. The translator's task, then, is to reproduce the source language's ostensive stimuli in order to achieve in the target recipients the same contextual effects as the source utterance has in the source language recipients. This understanding corresponds to the view that limits the expectations from the elusive equivalence to interpretive resemblance only.

Gutt's interpretive resemblance was adapted by Setton (2006) to be applied to simultaneous interpreting contexts. Setton argued that the linguistic repertoire available to the interpreter is always more limited, and the interpreter is fighting a losing battle against time while trying to find such stimuli that constrain the recipient's search for relevance in just the right way. The difference to transla-tion, in Setton's view, is that rather than trying to reproduce the communicative clues of the original (as a translator would), an interpreter is entitled to use the interaction of stimuli and context in any way that will deliver adequately similar effects, by whatever inferential route (Setton, 2006: 384). An interpreter must shape the context in which the audience will process their speech in order to compensate for distortions forced on it by the simultaneity condition (Setton, 2006: 384).

Also adopting relevance theory and interpretive resemblance as its main theoretical underpinning, a fascinating study by Miskovic-Lukovic and Dedaic (2012) analysed the case of disputed translation of a discourse marker 'odnosno'. The study illustrated how during the war crime trials at the International Criminal Tribunal for the Former Yugoslavia, linguistic indeterminacy of this discourse marker (which may have either an explanatory or a corrective/reformulative function) led the interpreter to make varying target item choices. These choices changed the ideological implications of the utterances and could affect the judge's decisions.

Setton's work draws on relevance theory and is mostly cognitively oriented. In fact, a large share of pragmatic research has been driven by the interest in the time-related aspects of interpreting. This interest accounts for the cognitive-pragmatic research strand, which seeks to answer questions about mental structures and procedures, processing capacity, translator memory, ear–voice span, speed of input, and so on (Moser-Mercer, 2000; Setton, 2003; Defrancq, 2015). Notably less attention has been paid to the sociopragmatic aspects of interpreting: pragmatic interference and pragmalinguistic transfer, the necessity for pragmatic adaptation, or the implications of diverging background knowledge among the speaker, the interpreter and the audience. The existing research on these topics is reviewed below. In Section 7.3 of this Element, we map out the blank areas where future research can be directed.

3.3 Participation Framework

Since the activity of interpreting serves the primary purpose of enabling communication among participants in a speech event, configurations of those participants have implications for pragmatic processes and choices. Research into the participation structure of interpreting gained traction after Wadensjö (1998) proposed her 'dialogic discourse-based interaction' model. It focused on the roles of participants in an interpreter-mediated event, the responsibility in distribution of content and progression of talk. The model adapts Erving Goffman's (1981) classic proposal regarding the speaker roles in a conversation that incorporates an author, a principal and an animator. An author is the party who composed the words of an utterance, a principal is the party whose views and beliefs are represented in the utterance and an animator is the sounding box: the person and/or the technology through which the utterance is made.

Wadensjö observed that the interpreter's role in an interaction is more than a mere transfer of meaning (stepping beyond the role of an animator), and, moreover, that interpreters co-construct meaning together with other parties. In Wadensjö's (1998) adaptation, the animator becomes the reporter, the author becomes the recapitulator and the principal becomes the responder. Thus, an interpreter who just reports a literal translation of what has been said takes the role of a reporter; an interpreter who is an active listener and not only renders but also understands the message is a recapitulator; and the role of responder is given to a participant who engages in order to respond, to take communication further (as an interpreter may sometimes do when asking a clarifying question).

Goffman's framework and Wadensjö's adaptation of it have become a productive tool of analysis of interpreting events and the interactants' understanding of their roles, especially in community (non-professional) interpreting. Some examples of such studies are Van de Mieroop (2012) or Keselman et al. (2010). Van de Mieroop (2012) recorded four doctor–patient interviews in a Flemish hospital, mediated by a community interpreter between Russian and Dutch, to study the quotative 'he/she says that'. She found that quotatives facilitate a switch in participation frameworks from the one where the doctor and the patient interact with each other to the one where the doctor and the interpreter are primary interactants. A similar shift in the interpreter's role from a mediator to negotiator was documented by Keselman et al. (2010) in twenty-six asylum hearings with minors (mediated between Russian and Swedish). A special issue wholly devoted to exploring how various factors in dialogue interpreting affect participation (Biagini et al., 2017) identified common ground as a factor in the degree of participation management that is required of interpreters (Ticca & Traverso, 2017) and questioned whether the interpreter is perceived as a ratified participant (Licoppe & Veyrier, 2017).

These findings from community interpreting contrast sharply with the behaviour of Pavel Palazhchenko, a professional and highly experienced interpreter who was the personal interpreter for former president of the Soviet Union Mikhail Gorbachev (Wadensjö, 2008). The study, analysing an American talk-show interview, found that the interpreter consistently resisted all attempts by the host to engage him as a responder. Instead, he participated in the event as a recapitulator and reporter only. When the host produced a side sequence addressed to the interpreter, Palazhchenko translated the utterance rather than replying to it, which Wadensjö construes as evidence of his high professional standards. This is one of many examples in which researchers assume that the invisibility of the interpreter is the quality benchmark for translation as communicative activity. On the whole, the participation studies of interpreting find that an interpreter can choose to have a certain degree of control over the interaction. The investigation of interpreter-constructed meaning will be taken up further in research on relational work and discursive identity, to be discussed in Sections 3.5 and 5.

A phenomenon frequently studied in classic pragmatics, deixis, provided another gateway to the investigation of participant roles in interpreting events. Deictic expressions point to the referents and rely on contextual information regarding speaker identity to be understood (Levinson, 2004); we typically rely on the visual cues in the physically co-present situations to know which discourse participant is referred to by 'I' or 'you'. Personal pronouns, a type of deixis, can indicate what assumptions about participant roles the participants in an interpreting event hold.

Disambiguation of deixis is a highly problematic topic in legal linguistics, and it comes as no surprise that interpreting studies have paid special attention to personal pronouns in court interpreting. One such study is described in Angermeyer (2005a), who looked at interpreted hearings in a small claims court in New York City. Angermeyer first established the institutional norms for interpreting in the American legal system; these norms presuppose that an interpreter is no more than a 'faithful sound amplifier' (Glémet, 1958) and therefore always interprets in the first person (direct speech). For example, if a defendant says in a foreign language 'I was going', the interpreter is expected to translate 'I was going' and not 'He said he was going'. In fact, interpreting in the third person is considered unprofessional (Pöchhacker, 2004: 151–2).

Angermeyer's (2005a) study aimed to find whether the interpreters in the small claims court used the first person (direct speech) or the third person (indirect speech). He discovered significant individual and directionality-related differences among his six interpreters with regard to this choice. Angermeyer put forth a hypothesis that the third person in interpreting is used to distance oneself from the speaker's words and identity.

The study of reported speech, and the identity role assignment it explicates, gained momentum in court interpreting (since it is important to be able to assign agency before assigning blame). Cheung (2012) and Cheung (2014) are examples of studies focusing on pronoun choices of court interpreters in Hong Kong. However, agency and participant roles can come into play in other domains as well, for instance, political meetings (Zhan, 2012) or international conferences on such disparate subjects as publishing and floral art (Chang & Wu, 2009). The studies have in common the finding that interpreters may choose to diverge from translating in the first person and close to the original's words in order to achieve successful mediation, since interpreter-facilitated communication is often charged with sociocultural factors. Indeed, Meyer (2008: 105–6) suggests that intervention may well be one of the very few true translation universals, that is, that interpreters are always actively involved in construction and adaptation of the target text rather than being mere sounding boxes. Research shows that complex pragmatic processes are involved in the resolution of vague deixis, especially personal pronouns (for example, first-person plural pronouns used for persuasive purposes to encode different group memberships). It is inevitable that interpreters will actively introduce pragmatic shifts since they become involved in the setting up of 'worlds of experience' (Chafe, 1980) or 'mental spaces' (Fauconnier, 1985) among the discourse participants using linguistic means to do so (e.g., dexis).

3.4 Politeness Research

A discussion of pragmatic research in interpreting would be woefully incomplete without addressing the topic of politeness. Politeness has been a major concern in pragmatics since the 1970s, first gaining traction with the theories describing strategic conflict avoidance and face-saving (Lakoff, 1973; Leech, 1983; Brown & Levinson, 1987). The elegance and relative simplicity of these theories made them a favourite among interpreting studies scholars looking to explore the issues of face-saving and mitigation in interpreting events. The very early studies in pragmatics of interpreting do indeed use Brown and Levinson's theory, for example, Knapp-Potthoff and Knapp (1987), investigating non-professional interpreting in German and Korean.

Given the body of work on the cross-cultural difference in mitigating politeness (e.g. the Cross-Cultural Study of Speech Act Realization Patterns (CCSARP) project, Blum-Kulka & Olshtain, 1984), scholars have been looking for the pragmatic shifts initiated by the interpreter on the basis of such cross-cultural mismatches. The study by Jacobsen (2008), also discussed in Section 3.2, for instance, traced the down-toning of face-threats to the fact that the face concerns of the Chinese defendants were likely to be different from the Western European face concerns of other participants. Courtroom and other official settings are a fertile ground for strategic politeness research due to a stable, easily controlled situational context of interactions: some of the many studies from these settings adopting Brown and Levinson's framework include Mason and Stewart (2001), Lee (2013) or Pöllabauer (2007). All of these essentially focus on how an FTA is rendered by interpreters (mitigated, aggravated or unchanged) in different language pairs and relative power configurations. Similar work has been done in other contexts of consecutive or liaison interpreting, for example, televised political debates (Savvalidou, 2011), or as experimental studies (Berk-Seligson, 1988).

In research on conference interpreting, facework and mitigating politeness received little attention, presumably due to the overall scarcity of research on this interpreting mode. The key contribution is Bartłomiejczyk's (2016, 2020) work devoted to the analysis of interpreting in the European Parliament using the concept of face and focusing predominantly on how mitigation is performed. It remains an excellent resource for anyone interested in a thorough overview of literature on strategic politeness research in interpreting. Magnifico and Defrancq (2017) also adopted Brown and Levinson's framework (and its extension, Culpeper's (1996) impoliteness framework) to analyse gender-based differences in impoliteness treatment by interpreters. Although the study's initial hypothesis is based on an outdated and deterministic view of male and female speech habits, the findings are interesting as they shed light on the different sensitivity to professional norms by male and female interpreters (female interpreters appear to be more preoccupied with faithful translation close to source, while male interpreters take more liberties with the text and foreground their role as mediators).

3.5 Relational Work

Although in the last two decades a shift occurred in linguistic politeness theory from strategic politeness approaches like Brown and Levinson (1987) to the all-encompassing analysis of facework like Spencer-Oatey (2000) or Locher and Watts (2005), these shifts found almost no reflection in interpreting studies. While the former approaches assumed a more or less stable form-to-function correlation between linguistic resources and their polite function, the latter, like the discursive approaches to relational work, argue that linguistic resources acquire their meaning in context through negotiation of societal norms. This, of course, makes such theories less convenient and straightforward to apply to language data, although naturally they boast much improved descriptive adequacy that reflects the fluid and messy nature of human communication. Nevertheless, a few studies of interpreting have taken the leap to incorporate relational work in their analysis, with interesting results, and demonstrated that it is a feasible step to take.

Some of this research has been carried out by Mapson (2015) on the material of sign language interpreting. Sign language interpreting is closest to liaison and conference interpreting in terms of temporality and participant structure, although the multimodal component is the crucial difference between the two (sign language interpreting being an intermodal interpreting type).

Mapson (2015) worked with data from general-purpose British Sign Language interpreting. Having facilitated and videorecorded several group interviews with eight experienced interpreters, she analysed the transcripts to identify the main politeness-related themes that emerged in participants' discussions. Mapson relied on Spencer-Oatey's (2000) rapport management framework to identify the types of facework that could be relevant to interpreters, for example, *smoothing* of interpersonal relations. The recognition of politeness has emerged as a prominent rich point, which highlights again the necessity of using the contextually aware politeness approaches, since form-to-function politeness theories would remain entirely blind to this problem.

Mapson (2015: 209) also highlights how interpreting (im)politeness essentially constitutes intercultural rapport management between the hearing and the deaf community. This makes interpreting especially difficult because interpreters are managing rapport between clients whose assessments of cultural norms may contrast. The interpreters' choices of what smoothing strategies to use in their target language output depends on a number of factors, not least of which is the pre-existing familiarity with the clients. The role of contextual awareness (Spencer-Oatey & Franklin, 2009) of the clients emerged as the key factor in interpreting politeness.

In a similar set-up, Mapson and Major (2021) collected data in group interviews with British Sign Language interpreters on the role of (im)politeness in interpreting. This was complemented by a second data-collection round that involved recording naturally occurring and role-play interpreting events in Australian Sign Language and English. All of the data came from the healthcare context, as Mapson and Major (2021: 63–4) believe the issues of politeness and rapport between a patient and a clinician are especially important for health outcomes and patient well-being.

The study relies both on the concepts of rapport management (Spencer-Oatey, 2000) and on relational work (Locher & Watts, 2005) to describe how sign language interpreters do interactional management. The rationale for the study was that *relational work*, 'the "work" individuals invest in negotiating relationships with others' (Locher & Watts, 2005: 10), is crucially dependent on the familiarity among conversation participants. This familiarity in turn affects the interpreters' ability to engage in *rapport management* with and between the clients: managing harmonious and smooth relations between people (Spencer-Oatey, 2005b: 96).

The findings describe previous interactions and shared knowledge among participants as a key component in successful interpretation of content and in the management of interpersonal relationships. In fact, in the interviews, interpreters highlight familiarity as a prerequisite for a satisfactory interpretation: 'The way I would voice it would depend on what I knew had happened previously, so their relationship with their manager, or mate, or whatever' (interview excerpt from Mapson & Major, 2021: 68).

Such familiarity lowers the cognitive load during interpretation sufficiently for the interpreter to be able to focus on mediating the relational work between the clients.

3.6 Summary

The main takeaway from these first forays of interpreting studies into the area of relational work is that the broader understanding of facework, and the ties it offers to discursive identity construction, is an invaluable way to make sense of the pragmatic choices the interpreters make. Indeed, it can make visible the contextual factors at play that hitherto remained outside the scope of mitigation-focused approaches. The case study in Section 5 of this Element offers a detailed example of an analysis that strives to understand simultaneous interpreting data through the lens of relational work and discursive identity construction. In Section 6, the study of relational work is revisited in a translation context.

4 Audiovisual Translation through the Pragmatic Lens

4.1 Introduction

We have already outlined in the introduction that, at the time of writing, pragmatics in translation is not yet an established discipline, but it is an area of study within linguistic pragmatics and within translation studies that is gaining traction. AVT was similarly described as an 'area of research that has to find its rightful place in Translation Studies' (Varela, 2002: 1), but quickly accumulated such a large number of research articles under its label that Remael (2010) suggested we may soon witness an audiovisual turn in translation studies. This statement is questioned by Pérez-González (2019) only with respect to the term 'turn', whereas he, too, emphasises the vitality and abundance of research projects that have been endeavoured in the field. In contrast to the overall interest in AVT and its translation processes and products, subtitling, dubbing and other modes of AVT (e.g. surtitling, voice-over, remakes) have only recently caught the eye of pragmatics researchers and are still an under-researched niche in the area of study we outline in this Element (see Desilla, 2019).

In what follows, we will first outline some general considerations regarding pragmatic research on AVT (Section 4.2), before moving on to a theorisation of the communicative settings and participation structures of different modes of AVT (Section 4.3), where we put the main focus on subtitling. Section 4.4 will then outline aspects of politeness and more broadly relational work that should be considered in future research. We return to audiovisual translation in Section 6, where we explore relational work in subtitles and viewer comments to Korean TV drama.

4.2 Pragmatics and Audiovisual Translation

More so than other areas in translation, audiovisual translation can be separated into specific translation practices and products, of which subtitling and dubbing undoubtedly have received most scholarly attention. As Section 4.3 will highlight, different modes of AVT also take place in different participation frameworks and therefore give rise to different pragmatic effects. These effects are crucial to the understanding of the translator-side production processes as well as to the viewer-side reception processes that constitute meaning-making in and of translated audiovisual artefacts.

When it comes to the existing theorisation and empirical study of AVT texts, it is useful to make a distinction between AVT approaches that focus on pragmatics and pragmatic approaches that focus on AVT. Given that translation studies is predominantly a contrastive discipline that prototypically works within a cross-linguistic paradigm, it is no surprise that cross-cultural approaches to AVT have been one focus of study. Predominantly, this approach has focused on text or text parts that were extracted and thus isolated from their multimodal context. In this vein, Guillot (2010: 88) emphasises that subtitles can be understood 'as a system of multimodal textual representation' with its own mode of interpretation. Subtitling and dubbing, she argues, are thus 'codes in their own right' (Guillot, 2016: 298). While this approach can shed light on pragmatic differences between source and target texts, and despite the fact that translation is at least implicitly understood as recontextualisation in the sense of House (2006), a conceptualisation of the 'pragmatic underpinnings of AV and AVT language' (Guillot, 2016: 298) is still missing. A complete picture of the pragmatic aspects of AVT would incorporate the full context of the recontextualised target text (see also Guillot, 2017). Inputs have been provided by the pragmatics of fiction, where the communicative setting of untranslated film has been theorised (see e.g. Bubel, 2006, 2008; Brock, 2015; Messerli, 2017; Locher & Jucker, 2021) and first steps have been taken to understand the reception situation of AVT artefacts (e.g. Messerli, 2019, 2020; Locher, 2020; Locher & Messerli, 2020; Messerli & Locher, 2021).

The advantage of conceptualisations within pragmatics has been freedom from the constraint of comparison that by definition informs any translation approach. A fruitful avenue in this regard seems an interdisciplinary return to the contrastive study design and contrastive pragmatic approach in which meaning-making in reception situations in intracultural and intercultural settings are juxtaposed. A crucial addition to this perspective will be the inclusion of multiple particular viewing situations – e.g. alone in front of a computer, together with a movie theatre audience or pseudo-communally with other viewers online (see Section 6) – and an understanding of their respective contexts and their consequences for the viewers' co-construction of meaning.

4.3 Participation Frameworks of Audiovisual Translation

Perhaps the most crucial contribution pragmatics can make to those practices traditionally examined by research in audiovisual translation is understanding these practices as language use in context. Such an approach would entail the systematic inclusion not only of utterances in comparison to the utterances they are translated from, but also of the surrounding communicative setting and in particular the participation structures that shape this form of situated language use. An obvious start for this endeavour is the understanding of the settings of film and television reception as they have been theorised in the pragmatics of fiction. Crucially, the collective sender – the conglomerate of all those involved in the production of audiovisual artefacts (Dynel, 2011) – communicates with the viewership via a multimodal fictional plane. Typically, the core events on that plane are interactions between characters played by actors and positioned in particular ways by the telecinematic processes, including the mise en scène. The viewers are, naturally, the primary ratified participants of this form of communication, but the conventions of fiction place further demands on these participants. The viewers are not only meant to suspend their disbelief and engage in joint pretence (Clark, 1996) that the characters and events are more than meets the eye and camera, but also to submit themselves to some degree of transporta-tion (Kuijpers, 2021) that positions them close to the scenes on screen as a type of bystander to the diegetic (story world internal) action. We will return to a particular example of the constellation of participants that shape (active) reception of a translated audiovisual artefact in Section 6.

For dubbed films, the deletion of source dialogue and its exchange for translated spoken dialogue means that reception processes remain relatively unchanged: viewers of dubbed as well as of original audio films listen to spoken dialogues in a multimodal context and understand, infer and co-construct meaning. Dubbing resembles text translation (Section 2) and interpretation (Section 3) in a number of interesting ways. It shares with both that its source and target texts are in the same mode and text type (spoken dialogue to spoken dialogue) and it shares with literary translation that it needs to be placed relatively close to the covert end of the overt/ covert translation continuum (Section 2.3; House, 2006). Dubbing typically hides, rather than advertises, that it is a product of translation. Arguably, however, the composite signal of multimodal audiovisual texts has a more significant non-linguistic component than is the case in literary translation. Malmkjaer (1998) understands the literary text as the sole point of contact between a writer and a reader, and considers one aspect of translation to be that it severs the connection, replacing it with a more indirect communication mediated by the translator. If we understand AVT in similar terms, then only the spoken dialogue is replaced and the connection between collective sender and viewer is only partially mediated via translator, whereas the rest of the multimodal signal remains a direct connection between the two. Accordingly, the prototypical stance the viewers of dubbed films undoubtedly take – that they are watching *the* film or perhaps a dubbed version of *the* film – is perhaps more justified than that of those readers of literature who only ever directly engage in communication with the invisible translator of the book they are reading.

At the same time, the difference in semiotic modes by which films and written texts communicate means that differences between source and target text in audio-visual translation are typically more pronounced on the level of language due to a set of particular constraints – e.g. lip synchronicity in dubbing. In dubbing, these differences also extend to the level of performance: while the visual aspects of actor performance are retained, the voice is substituted for that of a voice actor in the target language and culture. We cannot discuss the ramifications of these differences in full here, but it is clear that they will affect context in the sense of a recipient-side mental model of the situated performance and thus the inferential processing by which target text viewers make and negotiate meaning.

Subtitling, on the other hand, is at first glance a more overt translational practice since the presence of an additional layer (manifest in white writing on top of the film image) and the requirement for a different type of processing (reading) are constant reminders that viewers are engaging with an artefact that has been translated and that is linguaculturally 'other'. Moreover, the transfer of meaning from the spoken dialogue as source text – which is still present in the target text but at least partially inaccessible to target audiences – to written subtitles is a form of 'diagonal translation' (Gottlieb, 1994), with subtitlers mediating between source and target cultures based on a nearly identical film context and differing reception situation contexts (see Messerli, 2019).

Subtitles do not attempt to recreate the entire text but only the main linguistic aspects, and most typically the spoken dialogue. This fragmentariness of sub-title translation requires a re-evaluation of the notion of overtness/covertness and the differing inferential processes (Gottlieb, 1994; House, 2006). Of course, neither dubbed nor subtitled films are as covertly translated as, say, user manuals and other functional texts, for which we can postulate a readership that will process them as original texts. Overt translations, on the other hand, do not purport to be originals, but communicate explicitly on behalf of an original and provide access not only to its meaning but also to its context and textuality. Whether or not a source text is translated overtly or covertly is a pragmatic question dependent on the context, or rather contexts, of translation. It is clear that aspects of the source text influence its aptness for overt or covert translation, as do the influence of the recipients for which the translation is designed. Moreover, further modalities of the translation process also play a role in the relationship between translator, target text, author, source text and both source and target contexts that a translation establishes.

For instance, subtitling puts comparatively more emphasis on its status as translation than dubbing, and it is thus more overt, but when considering not only the subtitle text, but the subtitled film as a composite multimodal text, it, too, pretends to be not an original, but *the* original, text. After all, cinematic epitexts (Genette, 1997), such as the film listings at cinemas or the landing pages of streaming providers, do not present, say, the French subtitling of *Arrival*, but simply Denis Villeneuve's film *Arrival* as one single text, with dubbing tracks and subtitling texts as optional add-ons selected by cinema providers or streaming users. This is important because it positions subtitles as ancillary texts that serve as scaffolding for target audiences who make inferences about *the* film based on what the subtitles tell and show them about it. Agency for these texts can be attributed to the texts themselves – as a type of textual agency in the sense of Cooren (2004, 2008) – but also to the characters, the subtitlers or, more broadly, the collective sender (Messerli, 2019, 2020).

An additional aspect for the inferred (multiple) authorships of AVT texts is the relationship between translators and viewership. Irrespective of where agency is assigned, in a traditional professional setting, dubbed and subtitled texts necessarily communicate from a distance, from outside the viewing community they address. Audiovisual fan translations, most typically realised in the form of fansubbing, on the other hand, are community-internal translations that allow for the rest of the community to have influence and perhaps even adopt partial ownership of the translation (see Locher & Messerli, 2020 for examples of fans addressing fansubbers in viewer comments). Reading subtitles as explanations volunteered by another member of an in-group or as professionally produced translation each come with their own set of meaning-making processes, which also become manifest in the linguistic features of the subtitles (see e.g. Massidda, 2015).

What all forms of AVT texts have in common is the multiplicity of modes they are composed of. This characteristic brings with it the requirement for particular viewer literacies and the prompting of specific reception processes. We address the implications of these settings for relational work in Section 4.4, and we provide a more holistic account of meaning-making and relational work in a concrete case study in Section 6.

4.4 Relational Work and Audiovisual Translation

We have provided overviews of research on politeness and relational work in Sections 2.4 and 3.4 and will only offer a brief definition of the most central terms before moving directly to research in AVT and aspects particular to AVT texts.

Politeness has been studied in pragmatics first as marked behaviour specifically performed by speakers to mitigate face-threatening acts. The seminal work by Brown and Levinson (1987), easily applicable to different types of data, and more generally classic pragmatic approaches that treat individual linguistic actions as entities that are detachable from their interactional and other contexts (e.g. traditional speech act theory) still dominate the politeness research on AVT text. As is the case for interpreting studies (Section 3.4), interpersonal pragmatics and discursive approaches to (im)politeness have not yet made great inroads into the understanding of translated film and television.

A classic speech act approach to politeness is offered by Bruti (2006), for instance, who focuses on compliments in subtitling, positioning her findings in terms of positive and negative politeness. As is typical for the pragmatics-in-AVT perspective, she contrasts source and target texts both descriptively and evaluatively, finding that in compliments even more so than in the case of other speech acts, subtitle translation practices lead to pragmatic loss in some cases and are more faithful in others. A similar study based on the Pavia Corpus of Film Dialogue compares compliments and insults in original English and dubbed Italian language and finds no unambiguous patterns that would differ between the two, but crucially closes by pointing to the importance of context, advocating a shift from traditional microscopic politeness approaches to general aspects of interpersonal politeness (Bruti, 2007).

Despite this call for studying relational work more generally, most subsequent studies on politeness have focused on individual speech acts in relatively small examples of dubbing and subtitling, such as further studies on compliments in subtitles (Bruti, 2009), greetings and leave-takings in Italian dubbing (Bonsignori et al., 2011, 2012; Bonsignori and Bruti, 2015), directives in English and Spanish film scripts and subtitles (Pablos-Ortega, 2019), or requests in Italian dubbing (Napoli, 2021). More general accounts are provided, for instance, by Hatim and Mason (2000), who find a reduction of interpersonal markers in English subtitles beyond what would be explicable by spatio-temporal constraints (see also Oksefjell-Ebeling, 2012), and Gartzonika and Şerban (2009), who apply Brown and Levinson's framework to English subtitles and find no conclusive pattern in terms of the lowering or raising of face-threatening acts.

A more contextualised account has been provided by Pavesi and Formentelli (2019), who find that Italian dubbing employs hybridisation to mediate between source and target culture contexts and allow for target viewers to receive insults in a foreign language in particular and communication in general by exploiting pragmatic similarities in source and target languages. Finally, Locher (2020) shows how fansubtitling from Korean to English displays awareness of cultural and genre norms and the resulting pragmatic challenges for translation.

One very promising and largely unexplored research avenue is the multimodal pragmatic perspective Mubenga (2009) lends to requests and apologies in English subtitles. While he describes the process as tedious and time-consuming, the incorporation of ideational, interpersonal and textual levels in visual semiotic, functional grammatical and cognitive analyses of two examples from Godard's *Pierrot le Fou* manages to provide one of the most accurate and complete accounts of a contextualised AVT speech event published to date. Mubenga's (2009) own study does not directly correspond to the study of relational work aspects as defined in this Element, but applying a more discursively oriented multimodal pragmatics to larger data samples of subtitling and dubbing could provide insights into relational work as multimodally emergent in AVT discourse.

Mubenga's findings chime in with the work Sidiropoulou (2021) does on (im)politeness in AVT from the relational work perspective. Studying a minicorpus of English source film trailers and their dubbed and subtitled Greek versions, she finds that recipients appreciated the dubbed version's rendition of (im)politeness phenomena more. That rendition can be broadly described as the more domesticating option than that offered by subtitles, as the dubbed version adjusted culture-specific items, used orality features to reshape the interpersonal dimension between the addressees and invested more work into delivering the humorous implicatures to the audience.

4.5 Summary

This section has shown what pragmatic research avenues have been pursued in the study of AVT up to this date, while also pointing out promising starting points for future developments. Theoretically, we have advocated for transferring some insights from the pragmatics of fiction to a pragmatics of AVT, but also for interdisciplinary work. We have outlined some aspects of the participation frameworks that apply to different types of AVT, while acknowledging that no full account of the complex viewing situations of translated film and television has been provided to date. For the area of relational work, we have shown that there is a relatively large body of work on Italian subtitling and dubbing, but that these studies largely rely on mitigation-oriented politeness theory. Finally, we have shown some promising approaches that offer a more holistic understanding of reception contexts and a more situated understanding of relational work. In this vein, this Element moves on, in Sections 5 and 6, to two case studies which strive for more contextualised pragmatic accounts of particular aspects of interpreting (Section 5) and AVT (Section 6).

5 Conveying Risky Intent in Simultaneous Interpreting

5.1 Introduction

Theoretical background: the iceberg model of self-praise; relational work

Data: high-stakes political discourse in English and Russian, simultaneously interpreted

Research questions:
1. Do politicians and public speakers self-praise in the international arena in interpreted contexts?
2. Are any shifts in the amount of relational work introduced by the interpreters into the rendering of this speech act? If yes, are they towards positively or negatively marked parts of the continuum?
3. Are there any directionality effects in this process?

Simultaneous (or conference) interpreting is a cognitively challenging endeavour. Not only does it require the interpreter to perform all the tasks associated with translation – comprehending the input, finding an appropriate translation for an utterance and rendering it in a standard, fluent version of the target language – but this also needs to be done under extreme time pressure. In addition, the situational context is typically quite demanding as well, since conference interpreting is not provided in low-key everyday contexts but is reserved for important international events.

Moreover, the speaker and the target audience often come from vastly different cultural backgrounds. For example, the United Nations is a political body that routinely uses simultaneous interpretation across six official languages: Arabic, Chinese, English, French, Russian and Spanish, supplemented with relay interpretation for the speakers of other languages. This means that, theoretically, a report by a speaker from Afghanistan may need to be rendered to be understood by a speaker from the French territory of Wallis and Futuna (for the sake of the argument, the first and last members in an alphabetical list of the UN member states have been chosen here). To further complicate the task of the interpreter, it has been observed that some types of simultaneous interpreting might be oriented more towards the performative aspect of the target text (fluent, polished delivery) rather than the content-centred aspect (Kurz & Pöchhacker, 1995; Dayter, 2021a). Such a requirement places a high value on the interpreter's ability to render pragmatic phenomena such as politeness, degree of imposition, humour, hedging etc. across linguistic and cultural borders. The combination of the demanding cognitive environment with minimal room for deliberation, plus the requirement to produce a 'politic' (Locher & Watts, 2005) utterance for the target audience, make simultaneously interpreted language a fascinating subject to study via the pragmatic lens.

In this section of the Element, we describe the inner workings of a study focusing on just such a subject. Section 5.2 describes the choice of data, data collection and preparation. Section 5.3 presents the theoretical framework for the study and the research questions. Section 5.4 describes the methods, and Section 5.5 the results. Throughout the section, we also address the three key issues of mediality and participation structure (Section 5.2) and relational work (Sections 5.3 and 5.5). The section is in the large part based on the published work of one of the Element authors, Dayter (2021b). We turn to the study here in order to showcase the study design and methodological decisions and to illustrate possible research paths that involve relational work as an approach to analysing pragmatic phenomena in interpreting.

5.2 Data for the Study

Because simultaneous interpreting data is notoriously difficult to collect, there are not many openly available corpora that can be used for such a study. In this particular case, the decision was made to create a new specialised corpus; the creation procedure is described below. However, it is possible to make use of existing corpora, especially if the aim is to work with main European languages that are well-represented in existing collections. Some options available to researchers include the following:

- European Parliament Interpreting Corpus (EPIC)[2] is a corpus that contains nine language components: original speeches in English, Spanish, and Italian, each interpreted into the other two languages (Russo et al., 2012). It is available via the SketchEngine interface;

---

[2] https://docs.sslmit.unibo.it/doku.php?id=corpora:epic

- CoSi[3] is a corpus of simultaneous and consecutive interpreting of the German–Portuguese pair (Meyer, 2010); the web interface is open to the institutions that are members of the CLARIN consortium;
- DIRSI[4] is a corpus of simultaneous interpreting at medical conferences for English–Italian (Bendazzoli & Sandrelli, 2009) allows any user to submit queries and view the full transcripts and corresponding audio;
- SPARCLING[5] is a version of the Europarl transcript collection developed at the University of Zurich (Graën, 2018) that has been cleaned, structured in speaker turns, aligned on the sentence level and generally made suitable for linguistic research. It can be queried through the Multilingwis search engine.

For the present study, the corpus (dubbed SIREN, Simultaneous Interpreting Russian–English) has been collected via two main sources. The first source of data was the United Nations Web TV (http://webtv.un.org/). The website airs a variety of UN events such as General Assembly, press conferences, press briefings, etc., and conveniently stores recordings on the website for future use. The second data source comprises a variety of press conferences, briefings and interviews by Russian, American and British politicians and public figures that were broadcast with simultaneous remote interpreting on channels belonging to the video news agency Ruptly.

Mediality

Simultaneous interpreting in the United Nations typically happens in the following way: the interpreters sit in booths at the back of the auditorium, from which they can watch the proceedings while listening to the current speaker's voice over the headphones. The interpretation happens in the oral-to-oral mode, with the interpreter receiving auditory input and simultaneously producing voice-only output that will reach the audience through their headphones. Quite commonly, interpreters at the UN provide simultaneous-with-text interpreting, meaning that the interpreters are given the text of the speeches in advance and can use it for preparation and reference while interpreting. This adds a further input mode to the interpreter's source.

To supplement the simultaneous-with-text interpreting type with genuine free simultaneous interpreting, the second data source was used. The press conferences aired on Ruptly happen relatively spontaneously (compared to the UN sessions, where supporting documents are prepared weeks in advance) and are interpreted in oral-to-oral mode without sight translation. In contrast to the UN

---

[3] https://corpora.uni-hamburg.de/drupal/de/islandora/object/spoken-corpus:cosi
[4] http://cartago.lllf.uam.es/static/dir-si/dir-si.html
[5] https://pub.cl.uzh.ch/wiki/public/pacoco/sparcling

setting, the interpreter typically cannot see their audience (unless it is an international press conference, the interpretation is provided for the benefit of the audience of the Ruptly broadcast). This means that while the UN interpreters have an immediate visual feedback of the audience's reaction to their pragmatic choices, the Ruptly interpreters are working 'blind'.

Participation Framework

Again, the two data sources provide slightly different participant constellations. The United Nations events involve the in-house speakers, the interpreters and two layers of recipient audience: the portion of the in-house audience who require interpretation to understand the current speaker, and the spatially and temporally removed audience of the UN WebTV watching the broadcast. The in-house audience occupy the niche of the addressed participants, and the potential WebTV watcher is a bystander, in Goffman's terms (1981). In the case of Ruptly, the in-house audience is frequently absent, so the interpreter is working for the benefit of the TV watchers, who are therefore the addressed recipients, from the interpreter's point of view.

All in all, forty-one speech events were chosen from these two sources to represent a variety of situational contexts in the high-level political discourse in the international arena. The audio tracks from these events were transcribed using a simple orthographic transcription mode.

A useful tip for a creator of spoken corpora is given by Bendazzoli and Sandrelli (2005). They suggest streamlining the transcription process by training the speech recognition software Dragon Naturally Speaking to accurately transcribe the voice of the researcher, and then 'shadowing' the original recordings (listening to the recording in headphones and simultaneously repeating the words into a microphone). Dragon Naturally Speaking assisted with the transcription of the English part of the corpus. Unfortunately, no software of comparable quality was available for Russian, and the Russian part of the corpus was transcribed manually. As a final step, the transcripts were aligned on the level of utterance using the Nova Text Aligner, a simple text-aligning tool for Windows that allows one to export the data in .csv and .tmx formats. The .tmx files can be uploaded to the SketchEngine tool to create and query parallel corpora (although for the present study SketchEngine was not used). Information on the size and make-up of the SIREN version used in Dayter (2021b) is summarised in Table 1.

Table 1 SIREN size and make-up ('Total' counts an original speech and its interpretation as two separate speech events; SI = simultaneous interpretation)

Language component	N of speech events	Word count	Length
English original	16	69,697	483 min
Russian SI	16	41,262	483 min
Russian original	25	56,735	522.5 min
English SI	25	59,674	522.4 min
TOTAL	82 (41)	227,368	33.55 hrs

5.3 Theoretical Framework

The theoretical underpinnings of the study were twofold. First, the subject of the study was the realisation and the interpreting of self-praise. To shed light on the topic of self-praise, a perspective informed by the speech act theory and formalised in an 'iceberg model' was chosen. Second, to inform the understanding of the interpreters' choices regarding mitigation or aggravation of this potentially conflictual speech act, Dayter (2021b) relied on the relational work framework.

Self-Praise Iceberg

Self-praise is an interactionally risky behaviour that has been described by linguists and psychologists as violating the modesty maxim (Leech 1983), face-threatening (Brown & Levinson, 1987), taboo (Coupland, 1996) or psychologically maladaptive (Colvin et al., 1995). However, if we consider a purely linguistic definition rooted in speech act theory, no evaluation of appropriateness or desirability of communicative action needs to be present. Self-praise is 'an expressive speech act that explicitly or implicitly gives credit to the speaker for some attribute or possession which is positively valued by the speaker and the potential audience' (Dayter, 2016: 65). This definition mirrors the definition of praise or complimenting, a sister speech act well described in pragmatics (see Manes & Wolfson, 1981; Golato, 2005). Contrary to labelling it as maladaptive or taboo, the only interpretative step is the decision on whether the laudable attribute is positively valued by the interlocutors (this decision was taken on the basis of contextual knowledge about the particular political event and/or instrument underway; for example, when looking at a session of the Security Council of the United Nations, the analyst took into account the purpose of the specific session, as well as the overall stated UN goals, such as peacekeeping, and safety and security of the UN personnel). How self-praise relates to societal and community norms is a different issue that will be taken up in the subsection on relational work.

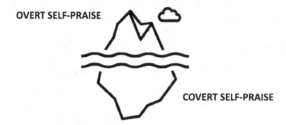

Figure 1 The self-praise iceberg (based on a figure in Rüdiger & Dayter, 2020)

The broad model of self-praise adopted in the study is the 'self-praise iceberg' (Rüdiger & Dayter, 2020; see also Figure 1). The metaphor captures the distinction between the explicit self-praise that is stigmatised in etiquette handbooks (i.e. it is visible above the 'water level' through meta-discourse) and the larger, but less visible, range of positive self-disclosures (i.e. the underwater part of the iceberg). The overall repertoire of self-praise available to speakers is divided into two portions. The 'above-water' portion of the iceberg encompasses overt self-praise, that is, the speech act of self-praise performed directly. The underwater portion, in turn, includes covert self-praise – the indirect speech act, performed by means of quoting the third party, couching self-praise in terms of complaint or sharing facts without evaluation. Performing self-praise covertly allows the speaker to avoid the epistemic contradiction inherent in positive self-disclosure. Pomerantz (1980) observed that self-praise involves a type 2 knowable: a statement about the speaker that is observable to others and is expected to be confirmed by an outsider. Along the lines of this argument, a self-praiser cannot evaluate type 2 qualities about themselves, for example being a persuasive and crafty speaker. Covert self-praise sidesteps this epistemic contradiction by presenting praise as stemming from a third party or based in incontestable, observable fact.

To illustrate this distinction with examples from Dayter's (2021b) study, example 5.1 is overt self-praise: it is an explicit statement about the speaker's exceptionality (who is the acting representative of the collective identity of America in this instance). The cue to count the statement as having positive value is the use of the adjective *exceptional* in combination with the positive connotations of investing efforts for the good of others. Example 5.2 is covert self-praise, as it contains a description of fact from which the audience needs to infer the speaker's (who is the acting representative of the collective identity of Belarus) positive qualities.

(5.1)   I believe America is exceptional in part because we've shown a willingness through this sacrifice of blood and treasure to stand up not only for own narrow self-interest but also for the interest of all.

(5.2) Belarus was among the few states who in 2012 provided an interim report on implementing the recommendations of the first UPR cycle.

Since covert self-praise often requires inference on the basis of shared knowledge, the underwater portion of the iceberg is largely specific to the community. The precise distribution of self-praise types across the iceberg – that is, their weightings in terms of appropriateness norms – depends on many different factors. The issue of appropriateness is theorised in the next section.

Relational Work and the Concept of Appropriateness

Much research to date has focused its efforts on questioning whether certain speech acts (for instance, self-praise) manifest in particular contexts where they might be expected to be avoided. This question can be reduced to asking whether the speech act is impolite (and therefore does not occur frequently) or polite (and therefore can be found in the corpus). Thus, studies proliferate on the material of different corpora, whereby it can be demonstrated that self-praise frequently occurs in some of them and is not to be found in others (Underwood, 2011; Wu, 2011; Speer, 2012; Dayter, 2016; Matley, 2017). This approach, informed by mitigation-oriented politeness theories such as Brown and Levinson's (1987), does not conclusively answer the question about the acceptability of self-praise because it cannot reconcile the occurrence of an unmitigated speech act with its face-challenging status. Such approaches to politeness assume that social capital or face is a zero-sum game: enhancing the face of one interlocutor means detracting from the face of the other. However, this is not the case in a wide variety of cooperative endeavours that humans engage in, where enhancing the face of the speaker contributes to the common goal of all interlocutors.

A more fruitful way of approaching the interactional status of self-praise is offered by a theoretical strand within interpersonal pragmatics, namely, relational work. Locher and Watts (2005: 10) propose that politeness is only a relatively small part of the relational work continuum, 'the "work" individuals invest in negotiating relationships with others'. The relational work framework covers a whole spectrum of behaviour, and steps away from the reductive polite/impolite dichotomy to make room for the behaviour that can be described in etic (i.e. theoretical) terms as a neutral, politic type of behaviour (see Figure 2). Politic behaviour is that which is appropriate to the ongoing social interaction (Watts, 2005) and needs not be negatively or positively marked. Politic behaviour is face-maintaining. In its marked form, politic behaviour can be assessed as face-enhancing and 'polite' from an emic (i.e. lay) perspective. When the speaker's and the addressee's background knowledge of interactional norms overlap sufficiently, they can remain in the unmarked zone throughout the interaction. If their

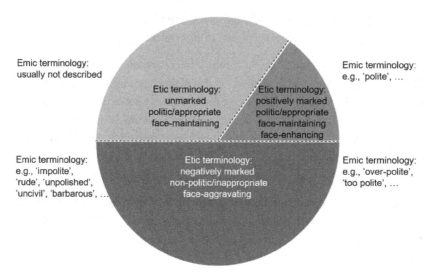

Figure 2 Relational work and its appropriate version (inspired by Watts, 2005: xliii)

perceptions of what level of relational work is appropriate to the ongoing interaction do not match, new norms of behaviour for the particular discursive practice may emerge as a result (Locher, 2006: 256). This discursivity between assessments of relational work is indicated with the broken lines in Figure 2.

Applying the relational work framework to the study of self-praise (im)politeness, we need not ask whether self-praising is polite or impolite in the high-stakes political context in Russian or English. The goal instead is to first establish what kind of relational work can be observed in connection with self-praise and then to explore what level of relational work the source-language speakers and the interpreters perceive as appropriate, and whether these levels match or are adjusted during the interpreting process. The study in this section therefore poses the following research questions:

1. Do politicians and public speakers self-praise in the international arena in interpreted contexts?
2. Are any shifts in the amount of relational work introduced by the interpreters into the rendering of this speech act? If yes, are they towards positively or negatively marked parts of the continuum?
3. Are there any directionality effects in this process, i.e. do interpreters introduce the same changes irrespective of the target language, or do they tailor their performance to the target audience?

5.4 Method

Similarly to the study reported in Section 6 of this Element, an investigation of relational work behaviours is fully dependent upon manual annotation. To make the process more efficient, the annotation was conducted in two rounds. In the first round, candidate instances of self-praise were extracted from the source-language subcorpora automatically using the queries identifying positive evaluation ('the best', 'the most', 'leading', 'winner', 'incredible', 'unique', etc. and their Russian counterparts). On the basis of distribution of these candidate instances in the corpus, high-density self-praise files have been identified, all belonging to the category of oral report in the Universal Periodic Review (UPR). The UPR involves a meeting of an intergovernmental working group of the Human Rights Council, which reviews the fulfilment of the human rights obligations based on the reports by the reviewed countries and third-party observers. In the second round, all corpus files belonging to this genre were manually annotated for instances of self-praise. In total, this resulted in 110 self-praise episodes in twelve speech events of the corpus.

For each self-praise episode, its corresponding translation was located in the aligned interpretation subcorpus and matched to the original excerpt. The utterance pairs (self-praise + translation) were saved in an Excel database and manually coded with regard to levels and markedness of relational work. The coding scheme had two levels. Level one, *translation of self-praise*, has three variants: no change (when the translation was judged to have the same amount of relational work invested in both languages); omitted (when self-praise was not interpreted at all); pragmatic shift (translation exhibited changes in the level of relational work). The variant *pragmatic shift* formed the second level of annotation, with two possible variants: mitigated (when the translation was judged to have more relational work, i.e. was more positively marked than the source); aggravated (when the translation was judged to have less relational work, i.e. is less positively or more negatively marked than the source). This kind of alignment was possible due to sufficient similarity between the two linguistic cultures in terms of interactional norms and pragmatic repertoires – a state of affairs that cannot be taken for granted, as the comparison between English and Korean in Section 6 will demonstrate.

5.5 Findings

Research Question 1

As the findings show, self-praise undoubtedly occurs in high-level political discourse (110 instances in the approx. 15 hours of spoken data – a descriptive statistic that does not indicate high frequency but nevertheless is well beyond what might be

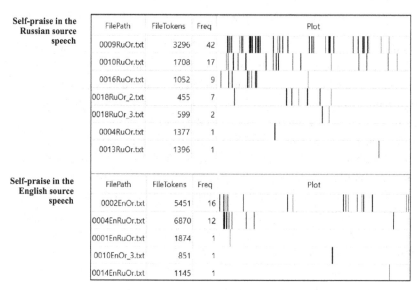

Figure 3 Concordance plots mapping the occurrence of self-praise in the corpus texts.

considered inappropriate or occasional). Figure 3 shows the distribution of self-praise across the two source-language subcorpora: it is noticeably more frequent in the Russian source files than in the English ones (seventy-nine episodes versus thirty-one episodes). The figure is created in AntConc 3.4 concordancer by searching for the self-praise tag manually added during annotation. However, one can see that a single file in the Russian corpus does most of the self-praise heavy lifting, with forty-two instances of self-praising behaviour in this speech alone, well above the number of hits in the other high-density oral reports (0010RuOr with seventeen hits, 0002EnOr with sixteen hits, 0004EnOr with twelve hits). It is an introductory statement by Valentin Rybakov, Deputy Minister of Foreign Affairs of Belarus, the head of the delegation responsible for submitting the Universal Periodic Review report on Belarus to the UN.

Seen from the angle of relational work, one may hypothesise that Rybakov's understanding of the interactional norm of the UPR report genre at the moment of this speech (in 2015) was different from the other actors. This offers an exciting research possibility for scholars of political discourse. Since Rybakov became the Deputy Minister of Foreign Affairs of the Republic of Belarus in 2013, and 2015 was a fairly early appearance in his United Nations career, the development of his linguistic behaviour and possible accommodation to the norm can be traced diachronically over at least seven years (he was named

Table 2 Self-praise instances and their interpreting in SIREN (from Dayter, 2021b: 34).

	Rendered fully in SI	Mitigated in SI	Omitted in SI	Total
Ru>En	46	28	5	79
	58%	35.5%	6.5%	100%
En>Ru	15	13	3	31
	48%	42%	10%	100%

the Permanent Representative of the Republic of Belarus to the United Nations in 2017 and remains in this post at the moment of writing).

Research Question 2

The findings show that the interpreters' renderings of self-praise realise all three possible outcomes: in some instances, self-praise is rendered without shifts in the level of relational work, but there are also many cases, up to 42 per cent in En>Ru interpreting, when the level of relational work is modified or self-praise is omitted altogether (see Table 2 for complete figures). In Wadensjö's (1998) adaptation of Goffman's production scheme (see Section 3 of this Element), in many cases the interpreters step out of the role of a reporter and become recapitulators by making changes to the original speaker's pragmatic choices.

Pragmatic shifts in the modified instances have all occurred in one direction only: towards mitigation (some translations included more relational work, i.e. were more positively marked than the source). Examples 5.3 and 5.4 illustrate such changes. Example 5.3 illustrates a typical case of the interpreter mitigating the original utterance by choosing weaker intensification, in this case changing the singular superlative adjective 'the best' to the collective form 'one of the best'. In example 5.4, self-praise is performed indirectly, as the speaker positions the United States as a unique benevolent force that no one else is capable of replacing. The interpreter modifies the original illocutionary force of the utterance and takes away the implication of uniqueness. In such cases, it is especially difficult to judge whether the interpreter made a conscious choice to adapt to the appropriateness norms of the target genre and audience or has simply failed to comprehend and render the implied meaning due to competing cognitive demands.

(5.3) Original   Беларусь имеет **лучший показатель** в регионе СНГ по уровню детской смертности

      Gloss   *Belarus has **the best indicator** in the CIS region in the level of child mortality*

      Interpret   we have **one of the best indicators** in the CIS when it comes to child and infant mortality

(5.4)   Original   the danger for the world is this that the United States after a decade of war rightly concerned about the issues back home // aware of hostility that our engagement in the region has endag- engendered throughout the Muslim world // may disengage creating a vacuum of leadership that **no other nation is ready to fill**

Interpret   *опасность заключается в том что США после десятилетия войн и будучи озабоченна внутренними проблемами могут наоборот отстраниться от решения любых вопросов в этом регионе // таким образом создастся вакуум который* **займут какие-то другие силы**

Gloss   the danger is that USA after decades of war and concerned with inner problems would on the contrary disengage from solving any issues in that region // thus creating a vacuum which **will be occupied by some other forces**

Research Question 3

There appears to be no directionality effect in the shifts of relational work between languages. Dayter (2021b: 40) reports that interpreters in En>Ru sub-corpora mitigate self-praise more often, but this difference is not statistically significant. If we focus on how self-praise is realised in each of the two source languages, Russian demonstrates a preference for explicit self-praise using strong intensifiers (superlative adjective forms such as 'the most responsible stake-holder', 'among the best 50 countries', 'one of the leading positions'). English speakers, on the other hand, use the base forms of adjectives, but the choice of the adjectives is more creative and descriptive (e.g. 'exceptional', 'incredible').

5.6 Summary

To conclude, the study found that the speakers in high-stakes political discourse frequently resort to overt self-praise using superlative adjective forms and creative self-elevating descriptions. The interpreters then render this self-praise fully, but also very often (in 35–42 per cent of cases) downgrade it in the target rendition, irrespective of interpreting direction. Mitigation-oriented theories of politeness, such as Brown and Levinson (1987), struggle to explain the contradictory conclusions. If self-praise occurs so frequently and in unmitigated forms, does this mean that it does not threaten the addressee's face and has a low degree of imposition? If that were the case, then why do the interpreters feel compelled to downgrade the intensifiers or flattering descriptions used by the speakers?

However, seen from the vantage point of relational work (and following the analysis in Locher, 2006), we can note that, simply because intensified self-elevation occurred, it does not mean that we have witnessed impoliteness. The overt self-praise is embedded into the context of reporting on a country's achieve-ments, warranted and indeed required by the genre. This explicit self-elevation is unlikely to be negatively judged by the audience and does not constitute nega-tively marked behaviour on the relational work continuum in Figure 2. It is well within the limits of what is perceived as politic, or appropriate, for the then-current norms of interaction. A useful exercise is to imagine a speaker who, while delivering their report for the Universal Periodic Review, minces words and coyly denies their country's achievements, creating a conversational opportunity for the chairman to contradict them. This would likely be recognised and interpreted as over-polite (and therefore inappropriate) by the delegates.

The interpreters, in turn, operate under their own current norms of interaction. Again, if the finding of the study is that the interpreters' renderings are a mix of full translation and downgrading irrespective of the language direction, we conclude that this is the interactional norm shared by the members of the profession. It is perhaps a self-fulfilling prophecy of sorts that translators and interpreters, who are taught the concept of translation universals and normalisation in their studies, come to believe that a translation is always more flat, less exuberant, than the source and realise it in their work. Whatever the case may be, occurrence of a behaviour and absence of any challenges or censure of this behaviour should be taken as evidence for its status as an interactional norm. The norm often becomes visible only when someone unfamil-iar with that norm joins the conversation and precipitates the creation of a rich point – an analytical angle that Section 6 of this Element will explore.

The study illustrates how the relational work approach to politeness can be productively applied to the analysis of pragmatic phenomena in translating and interpreting. It avoids the zero-sum game view of human interaction that underlies the mitigation-focused approaches to politeness and instead accom-modates a more flexible understanding of how interactional norms may differ among audiences or be negotiated in context. For example, in the context of the Universal Periodic Review, where the whole body of the UN presumably works towards upholding human rights, self-praising on the human rights topic con-tributes towards that joint enterprise (even while self-elevating over other countries through direct comparisons of successes may still be face-challenging). The interpreters may then actively navigate the speaker's and their own understandings of this interactional norm by making decisions about what constitutes a face-challenge and what enhances collective face.

The study has also identified other accessible interpreting corpora that can be used for further research (EPIC, CoSi, SPARCLING, see Section 5.2) and potential research directions, such as a diachronic analysis of a speaker's recognition of, and adherence to, interactional norms (for example, Valentin Rybakov's self-praising behaviour, as discussed in Section 5.5).

6 Relational Work in Korean Drama Subtitling and Live Comments

6.1 Introduction

Theoretical background: relational work, character and identity construction, participation structure

Data: scenes from fictional Korean TV dramas that contain moments of relational work; timed comments on episodes

Research questions:

1. Given the fact that negotiating relational work in Korean culture is pervasive, are such negotiations included in Korean TV drama artefacts?
2. How do lay subtitlers make scenes containing relational work negotiations accessible to non-Korean viewers?
3. Do viewers comment on relational work when viewing scenes containing relational work negotiations?

While translating fiction and researching the translation process has a long tradition, the use of fiction in pragmatics needs more explanation, especially when exploring (im)politeness ideologies with a relational work approach. Working with fictional data in linguistics itself is not new. For example, historical linguistics draws on language used in all types of written sources to document varieties in time and space and to research language change. Research in stylistics uses fictional data to explore different writing styles and meaning-making processes in readers and viewers, often working with pragmatic concepts. Research in historical pragmatics often explores dialogues from plays to study the use of address terms or speech acts, stating that the fictional dialogues are the closest we can get to interactional data in the absence of recordings. Rather than contending that fictional data is deficient because it cannot reflect face-to-face communication faithfully, we follow the argument that the language and interaction depicted in fictional artefacts such as TV series, movies, novels and plays are of interest for pragmatics exactly because it is included for effect (see Alvarez-Pereyre, 2011; Locher & Jucker, 2017, 2021; Messerli, 2021; Locher et al., 2023). Fiction in its various forms and understood as a cultural artefact is thus part of a society *as* naturally occurring data in its own right in the sense that analysts neither instigated nor influenced the creation of this data.

Fictional artefacts provide excellent data for discussing the staged manifest-ations of ideologies of a particular time and place. This general tenet is motiv-ated by the insight that texts are tied to their time and place of creation and create worlds in which norms of behaviour are reflected, contrasted and imagined in relation to this context. Even when the fictional text plays in future or past worlds (from the point of view of writing time), its effect will be partly derived from the contrast between the world of creation and the world of reading/ viewing. From the point of view of readers and viewers, it matters when they read a text (i.e. contemporary or past text), as they will interpret it from their own cultural background, which is tied to their present-existing norms and ideologies. When studying (im)politeness norms from an interpersonal prag-matics perspective, scholars are interested in evidence of relational work and the surfacing of ideologies in such texts, while keeping the potential mismatches between time of creation, time depicted within the artefact and time of reception in mind. In the case of translation, we can add the further challenge of engaging with a text that depicts ideologies that might be different from one's own if the cultural background is not shared. This point is illustrated in the research by Pollali and Sidiropoulou (2021), who describe how two different Greek trans-lations of the same play, made seventy years apart, discursively highlight different aspects of a character's identity depending on what concept of familial hierarchy and children's rights was relevant at the time of translation.

In fiction, characters are created though a multimodal combination of indexic-als that tap into ideologies and in their combined form are used for identity construction (see Locher & Jucker, 2021: chapter 6; Locher et al., 2023: section 5). Such indexical cues can be visual aspects including sex/gender, clothing or comportment (in enacted or described form), as well as linguistic (e.g. standard versus dialect features). For example, when dressed in designer clothes and made to speak with a posh accent and express themselves elegantly, characters can be interpreted as belonging to a particular class in society, endowed with particular status. This impression can be made more salient when such characters are contrasted to characters who lack these traits. Creating characters in fiction and positioning them vis-à-vis each other through linguistic and multimodal means is often plot-relevant. In addition, how characters are portrayed to adhere to, challenge or negotiate ideologies through behaviour depicted as (im)polite also adds to their overall character creation. This is because relational work and identity construction are interlinked (see, e.g., Locher (2008) for the connection between relational work and identity construction). In Figure 4, Ramos Pinto (2018: 24) nicely summarises how different modes work together to construct meaning and how positions are created within the artefact that can then be juxtaposed, reinforcing or contradicting each other. Relational messages can be

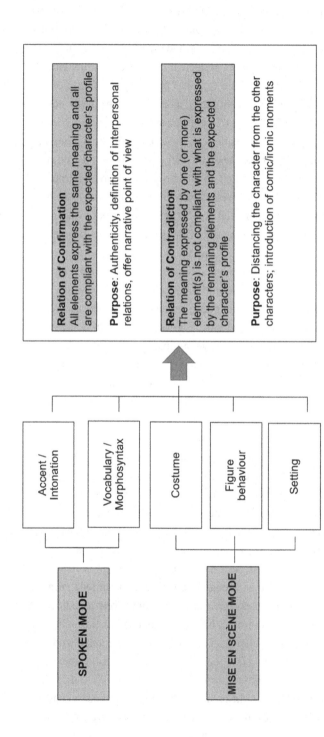

Figure 4 Formal elements to consider in the source product and possible multimodal relations (adapted from Ramos Pinto, 2018: 24)

tied to both modes listed and contribute to character creation and transporting ideologies around relational work.

Relational work in fictional telecinematic artefacts thus cannot be easily neglected or glossed over in translation processes. Translators face the challenge of aligning identity-building cues between different languages that come with different indexicals. Looking at Figure 4, many of the cues that signal relational work will not be translated at all in the case of subtitled artefacts. The spoken mode of the original is retained but complemented with a written translation; the viewers will likely not be able to pick up cues such as dialect features in the audio-track but, to a certain extent, they might pick up paralinguistic features such as urgency in tone. The mise en scène is retained and carries cultural indexicals that are, however, not commented on or translated but remain visible for interpretation (e.g., status symbols for clothing, bowing, etc.).

When considering the linguistic level, differences concerning relational cues exist between languages concerning relational cues. For example, there are different address term systems and uses of pronouns in different linguacultures. Depending on what choices translators make, the relational work effect created in the source text might change the character relations depicted in the target text. To be more concrete, using first names reciprocally when addressing each other might be indicative of closeness and solidarity in one language, while it might be more neutral or avoided in others. Moreover, translation provides a unique lens for teasing out such differences, as juxtaposing different representations of relational work in source and target texts is likely to reveal variation in perception of interpersonal relations in different reception environments, as e.g. work by Pollali and Sidiropoulou (2021) demonstrated.

This section showcases aspects of Locher and Messerli's work on subtitle fan translations of relational work in Korean TV drama (Locher, 2020; Locher & Messerli, 2020; Messerli & Locher, 2021) and also draws on our current continuation of the project. Korean is a language that indexes relational work cues in many different linguistic and embodied ways and thus serves well as an example of the challenges translators face. Rather than offering entirely new insights, we use our project as a springboard to showcase a number of pragmatic questions one can ask about our type of data. In what follows, we will first outline aspects of Korean relational work indexicals (Section 6.2) and discuss them in relation to translation challenges for the Korean–English pair (Section 6.3). In Section 6.4, we will then explain our data and our methodological decisions concerning how to study relational work in the fictional artefacts, and explore how we can tie the project to the study of relational work in Section 6.5 and to participation structure in Section 6.6. We will end the section with an outlook on remaining issues to be explored in Section 6.7.

6.2 Korean Indexicals for Relational Work

Korean has many linguistic cues available to perform relational work with an (im)politeness stance, including verb/adjective endings that indicate six different politeness levels, particular honorific morphemes that can be combined with these endings, a specialised lexicon that is used when addressing people of higher status, and a complex system of address terms that help position interlocutors vis-à-vis each other (for overviews, see Choo, 2006; King, 2006; Koh, 2006; Brown, 2011, 2015). Furthermore, aspects such as body posture, lowered eyes, bowing, hand position when pouring drinks, etc. all can be used to index positioning of the self vis-à-vis the other (Brown & Winter, 2019). The choice and combination of these cues is complex and informed by cultural ideologies derived from Confucianism, which gives value to a person's status within society. Factors shaping this status are many, from the importance given to birth, family and marriage to provenance, education, profession, financial wealth, age difference, social distance and seniority (see, e.g., Brown, 2011; Yuh, 2020).

Foremost, the verb and adjective endings in Korean always contain a relational positioning component that indexes one of six politeness styles (Brown, 2011: 1; Rhee & Koo, 2017: 101). There are thus no sentences that do not somehow make a relationship claim, since these endings indicate how the speaker stands in relation to the addressee. Importantly, the levels are negotiable and dynamic to a certain extent, and shifts can be observed within the same speech event (Brown, 2015: 305). When we link this observation to fiction and character construction, the Korean audience has many morphological cues to pick up on when reading or listening to characters' dialogue.

Korean is also a pro-drop language and, in addition, Koreans often avoid addressing each other by pronoun and by first name. Instead, a complex address term system is preferred which allows interactants to refer to each other in their function and role vis-à-vis the speaker. Examples derived from the family field are different terms for older brother and younger brother, depending on whether the speaker is a man or a woman. Examples from the workplace are a plethora of job titles. Distinctions between senior and junior are of relevance, for example, at the school, university or workplace.

In addition to verb/adjective politeness levels, address terms and specialised lexemes that are used when addressing people of higher status, Korean also has numerous lexical and morphological stance markers that can be drawn on to indicate to the addressees that a face-threatening act is being mitigated or enhanced.

In sum, Korean has a complex grammaticalised and lexicalised system of signalling relational work which is exploited in dynamic ways by its users for relationship creation. This complexity finds its way into fictional artefacts where, within a short span of time (in the case of telecinematic artefacts) or limited number of pages (in the case of written texts), fictional characters are created and relationships and their transformation performed and displayed.

6.3 Challenges for Translation of Korean Relational Work Indexicals

Plot-relevant positionings and negotiations of relational work by characters in Korean TV drama come with their own translation challenges. If we take the Korean–English language pair, English has no honorific morphemes, nor can it express different politeness levels through verb or adjective suffixes.

With respect to the lexicon, English has a plethora of near-synonyms that might differ in indexing a character's education status (refined versus unrefined ways of expressing oneself), or their wish to adhere to more or less formal registers or to breach linguistic norms (e.g. by using slang or vulgar expressions in contexts where formal standard speech would be expected). Characters can express regional, social or ethnic belonging through lexical and phonological features. Such nuances also exist in Korean. However, such refined indexicals are culture-bound and do not travel well from one language to another (see, e.g., Locher, 2017; Planchenault, 2017; Ramos Pinto, 2018). This is because the features carry different levels of prestige, and negative connotations are often associated with substandard varieties. In other words, these judgements are tied to cultural knowledge of the indexicals in the target language rather than the source language.

While this translation challenge is the same for most language pairs, the Korean lexicon furthermore has a set of lexemes for everyday items (e.g., 'rice/ meal': pap/밥 vs. siksa/식사; 'person': salam/사람 vs pwun/분; 'to sleep': cata/ 자다 vs cwumwusita/주무시다) that are used when addressing people of seniority and elders. To translate these terms merely with formal English terms will miss the nuance of respect as their Korean use is not limited to formal situations only.

With respect to address terms, English would either prefer first names or last names plus title in many cases where an analogy between Korean and English address terms might be possible. In other cases, there are no clear equivalents available and a descriptive translation might sound clumsy. For example, if a Korean character addresses their uncle, they will choose a term that indexes whether the uncle is maternal or paternal, whether this uncle is older or younger than the parent whose brother the uncle is, whether this uncle is married or not. All of this information with respect to the positioning of the character is available to the Korean audience but cannot be carried over into the simple English translation of 'uncle'.

To explain the translation pair Korean–English somewhat more, it should be stressed that similar challenges also occur in the opposite direction. When English texts are translated into Korean, translators have to position characters vis-à-vis each other in a level of detail that is not contained in the original texts (e.g. claims about seniority, age difference and relative status). This is because the obligatory Korean verb and adjective endings carry relational information and cannot be omitted. Depending on whether translators aim at domestication or foreignisation, they will engage in creative character construction, the degree of which is at the discretion of the translators.

To return to the Korean–English direction of translation, we can observe that a close translation of all the relational aspects is impossible and that there is an overall reduction in relational cues. While translators would thus have to aim for rendering a general pragmatic stance or tone, as has been argued by many scholars, such as Kiaer (2018) or House (2018a, 2018b), rather than aiming at an equivalence impossible to achieve, Korean and English nevertheless also share a number of similar relational work strategies. For example, lexical hedges exist in both languages (e.g. a little, co/좀), and many of the morphological stance markers that can be combined with verb/adjective endings can be translated with lexical hedges in English instead. In addition, the general idea that the longer the sentence, the more relational work is invested, holds for both languages.

In sum, translating linguistic relational work from Korean to English is challenging, but negotiations of relational work in Korean transport defining cultural ideologies that cannot simply be dropped entirely if the overall meaning of the fictional text is to be retained. This is especially the case when the aim is to also translate the 'Koreanness' of the source text. Such a trend to orient to foreignisation rather than domestication has been reported for fan subtitling in previous work (Tomaszkiewicz, 1993; Díaz Cintas & Muñoz Sánchez, 2006; Pettit, 2009).

6.4 Research Questions and Data

In what follows, we will illustrate a number of questions that we developed when engaging with Korean TV drama as viewers who are not speakers of Korean. In other words, we are interested in how culture-defining relational work moments can be recognised and how they are made accessible for an international viewership. Our research questions are:

1. Given the fact that negotiating relational work in Korean culture is omnipresent, are such negotiations included in Korean TV drama artefacts?

2. How do lay subtitlers make scenes containing relational work negotiations accessible to non-Korean viewers?
3. Do viewers comment on relational work when viewing scenes containing relational work negotiations?

It is important to point out that our work does not aim at establishing the accuracy of the English translation with respect to the Korean original, nor do we tally the 'loss' in indexical cues. The latter is an endeavour that is not a fruitful research path in the first place (see Section 7). Instead, we focus on the English subtitles in their own right (Guillot, 2020) and wonder how they, in combination with the retained audio-track and visual character information (action, appearance, language (Bednarek, 2011); spoken mode vs mis en scène (Ramos Pinto, 2018)), transfer information on relational work.

Our data stems from the online streaming platform Viki.com, which gives a global viewership access to licensed Asian dramas (with or without subscription). The translations into many different languages are provided by fans, who can use a built-in translation interface when translating. In addition, viewers can comment on what they see in so called 'timed comments,' i.e. comments that are displayed while a particular scene is playing. Our data consists of two corpora. For the subtitles we worked with 110 episodes from seven different dramas, which amounts to a corpus of 613,000 subtitled words in English (Locher, 2020; Locher & Messerli, forthcoming). In addition, we collected 320,118 timed comments for five of these dramas, which amounts to 2,910,258 words written by 33,309 users in thirty-six languages (with English being predominantly used in 50 percent of all comments (Messerli & Locher, 2021: 414)). The subtitles are open source and the timed comments are openly available even when viewing without subscription. We anonymise commenter usernames to ensure anonymity.

6.5 Insights on Relational Work Negotiations

In order to answer question 1, Locher (2020) had to define a unit of analysis. We decided to identify 'scenes' that contained instances of 'classificatory politeness1' or 'metapragmatic politeness1' (Eelen, 2001: 35). In other words, we worked with scenes where characters used lexical items from the semantic field of (im)politeness or where characters explicitly engaged in meta-discussions about (im)politeness. We termed such occurrences 'moments of relational work' and included the scene in which this moment occurred in our data to provide sufficient context. A scene could contain more than one moment of relational work.

As a case in point, consider example 6.1, which shows an extract from a scene where relational work is being negotiated on a number of different levels. The context is the first encounter between the two characters in the drama *One More*

Happy Ending. The male lead, Song Soo-Hyuk (SSH), is a reporter disguised as a heavily pregnant woman in order to pursue a celebrity who is visiting an OBGYN clinic. When parking his car, he bumped into another parked car and left his business card to alert the car's owner. When walking away from the car, the female owner, Han Mi-Mo (HMM), appears and they start talking.

(6.1)   *One More Happy Ending*, Ep. 1, start at 00:20:47, English subtitles from Viki (comments in brackets are in the original subtitles display)

	Character	Subtitle	Action description and comment
1	Han Mi-Mo	Excuse me, Ahjumma!	HMM is addressing SSH who is walking away from the car.
2		Oh my. What's this ...	Inspecting the cars.
3		Ahjumma! If you hit my car, you should compensate me.	HMM turns accusingly to SSH.
4	Song Soo-Hyuk	I am sorry.	SSH bows while apologising. HMM utters 'omo' (an expression of surprise) at the sound of SSH's deep voice, which reveals him to be a man.
5		I'm really sorry, but I have an urgent matter to tend to, so ...	Fast speaking, matter of fact.
6		I left my card on the car and I've also called the insurance company,	
7		so they'll be here soon to fix it. Please handle it when they do arrive.	SSH turns to leave.
8	Han Mi-Mo	No, no. Wait.	HMM prevents him from leaving by extending her arm to block his way.
9		What kind of accident is it that it's so informal?	HMM looks at him accusingly. SSH inhales impatiently.
10		Business card?	
11		Whether you are ahjumma or ahjussi ... How can I trust a person who speaks differently from what he looks like?	HMM refers to SSH pretending to be a woman.
12	Song Soo-Hyuk	Ajummoni.	SSH looks at her directly and confrontationally. The camera shows HMM taken aback at the choice of address term, with her jaw dropping. A sound effect (deep downward chime) signals that her uptake is negatively marked.

13		Have you ever seen a hit and run who has parked his car?	The camera oscillates between HMM and SSH, showing her outraged and disbelieving facial expression, while SSH is irritated at the hold-up and his sentence intonation displays displeasure.
14		That's why I am asking for your understanding, and I have an urgent matter to take care of, too.	
15	Han Mi-Mo	More than getting my car hit, that designation is pissing me off.	HMM chuffs twice before speaking.
16		Ajummoni?	Outraged. Disbelieving intonation. Accusing eye gaze.
17		Where do I look like an ahjumma?	While HMM speaks, SSH facial expression shows that he realises that HMM is offended but he is still irritated about this hold-up.
18		To hear 'ahjumma' from a person like you in broad daylight, do you think	
19		I am applying eye cream every night?	
20	Song Soo-Hyuk	I am sorry. I didn't recognise you Agassi (Miss).	SSH takes a deep breath and shakes his head somewhat, signalling giving in in an annoyed manner. He slightly hesitates before pronouncing Agassi sarcastically.

Example 6.1 is a scene that displays relational work being negotiated on many different levels. We see the contestation of address terms throughout the scene and meta-comments on formality (subtitle 9) in relation to expectations voiced about role-behaviour in such a car accident incident. We can also see that the multimodal cues, in addition to the lexical ones, help the viewers to understand that Han Mi-Mo is outraged at being addressed as Ahjumma (아줌마, 'common term for a married woman', Naver online dictionary), which she gives negative value and associates with being old (applying eye cream, subtitle 19). We witness Song Soo-Hyuk, who wishes to make a quick

exit and who reluctantly adjusts his use of address terms from Ahjumma to Ahjummoni (아주머니, which is more respectful) and then Agassi (아가씨, used for younger, unmarried women) in order to appease Han Mi-Mo and to bring the conversation to a close. His sarcastic tone when uttering 'Agassi' in subtitle 20 signals that he only pays lip-service to the situation while clearly not perceiving Han Mi-Mo as young.

With respect to the staging of relational work in this fictional scene, we learn about the importance of choosing the right address terms, and the fact that a woman who is no longer entirely young might feel offended at being addressed with a term reserved for older married women. With respect to the plot, this information is important since Han Mi-Mo runs a marriage agency for divorced people (being a divorcee herself) and one of the recurrent ideologies that is being played with throughout the drama is preoccupation with youth and wealth by the clients of the agency.

With respect to translation strategies, we can see that the fan subtitlers retained the Korean address terms and also added a comment in brackets to clarify the term 'Agassi (Miss)' (subtitle 20). Importantly, information on relational work is not only found in the lexical choices of the dialogue but crucially also in the visual comportment cues of the characters as well as the sound effects that accompany uptake (subtitle 12).

When creating our corpus, two coders watched and took stock of scenes similar to example 6.1 in 110 episodes from seven dramas. In response to research question 1, the general importance that Korean society gives to positioning is also reflected in televised Korean drama, which contains such moments of positioning in an average of 2.9 scenes per episode (323 scenes overall, containing 428 moments of relational work).[6] In response to research question 2, the moments of relational work could be classified into four types: '(1) character address term negotiations; (2) character meta-comments on relational work; (3) character meta-discussions on role understanding; and (4) subtitler meta-comments on language and culture' (Locher, 2020: 139).

The first three categories are more straightforward from a translation perspective because the characters themselves use lexical items around which relational work negotiations become salient. Usually, these scenes are several turns long, which means that the relational work entailed is given prominence for plot reasons and subtitlers need to engage with the scenes, too. The subtitler comments on language and culture are of particular interest to us because they show awareness of relational work cues. For example, address terms might be

---

[6] Locher (2020) reports 3.2 scenes per episode. This result was based on sixty-eight episodes from four dramas, while the results reported here are based on a larger corpus.

translated (see subtitle 20 above) or non-translatable grammaticalised cues are explained in brackets (e.g. 'I am a teacher. (formal)', OMHE, Ep. 14). Viewers are thus alerted to the linguistic relational work level and that something relevant for understanding characterisation is going on in the verbal track of the artefact.

In sum, we found that (a) by mere staged inclusion, the televised moments of relational work can help non-Korean viewers realise the importance and complexity of relational work negotiations in Korean culture, despite the typologically necessary reduction of linguistic relational work cues on the linguistic level in the subtitles, and that (b) the subtitlers function as cross-cultural mediators for the international viewership (Bassnett, 2012).

6.6 Insights on Participation Structure

Addressing research question 3 allowed us to revisit the notion of participation structure. Building on our insights that the fan subtitlers function as self-selected cross-cultural mediators by orienting to the source text in their translation efforts, we explored the contribution of the viewers to the artefact in timed comments since they, too, are adding their voice to the original multimodal artefact (see Figure 5).

In qualitative coding of all timed comments contained in the first and last episode of two dramas, Locher and Messerli (2020) discovered that viewers comment on many different aspects of the drama (artefact-oriented comments) and contribute to fandom community-building by engaging with each other (community-oriented comments). Displaying emotive stance was the function

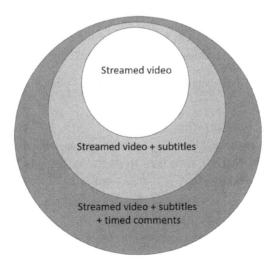

Figure 5 Nested, polyphonic voices on Viki (reproduced from Locher & Messerli, 2020: 25)

that timed comments performed most often, and this stance could be oriented to both the drama and the community.

With respect to Korean culture, we can state that the fan community displays their interest in the source culture by borrowing and using Korean words, exhibiting knowledge of Korean drama conventions, actors and other aspects of the Korean wave (such as knowledge of K-pop singers and bands), asking questions about Korean culture and comparing Korean cultural aspects to their own practices. Viewers who have timed comments activated when viewing are thus exposed to yet another voice that shapes the uptake of the original streamed video (see Figure 5).

We also explored whether viewers comment on relational work in particular (Locher & Messerli, 2020, forthcoming) and found that this does indeed occur but is not particularly frequent when looking at the overall distribution of what viewers choose to comment on. For example, the scene in example 6.1 receives many comments that display emotive stance in that viewers enjoy the humorous effect of the scene and the disguise of the male lead character as a pregnant woman (see example 6.2).

(6.2)   Selection of timed comments during example 6.1 illustrating emotional stance and the use of Korean borrowings

- LMAO … its not enough he's wearing a wig … but he is pregnant also …
  I cant breathe from laughing so hard . . ..
- Ahjumma 😂😂😂 what is he wearing 😂😂 I'm crying
- I'm dying 😂😂 she called him Ahjumma!!!!!!!
- LOL! Ahjumma!

In addition to the visual appearance in the form of disguise, the viewers also pick up on multimodal cues and thus show awareness of visual and auditory cues for character identity construction (see example 6.3).

(6.3)   Selection of timed comments during example 6.1 illustrating uptake of multi-modal cues

- His voice made her shake 😂😂😂😂😂
- omg he litreallly look like an ahjumma im laughing so hard
- AHHAHAHAHA IM DYING HES SO PRETTY BUT HIS VOICE.
  AHAHAH OH SHIT
- lmao moment when you think its a girl but the man voice shows
- HER SHOCKED GASP LOL IM DYIN
- so hyuk literally looks like an old lady i love it

Throughout, the viewers use the term Ahjumma by either repeating the dialogue of the characters or using the term as referent themselves (examples

6.2–6.4). Viewers also pick up on the choice of address terms (6.3). They quote Han Mi-Mo's shocked reaction to being addressed as Ahjummoni ('omo'/oh my god), which is not in the subtitles, thus displaying a keen ear. And they make analogies of what the term Ahjumma might index in their own languages ('MA'AM'; 'vieja', that is 'being old' in Spanish).

(6.4)   Selection of timed comments during example 6.1 illustrating uptake of the marked choice of 'ahjummoni' in subtitle 12

   - ☺☺☺ 'omo'
   - Hahahahhahaha 'OMO' phahaha
   - You can call me bitch, but don't call me MA'AM! ROTFL . . .. she's wants to kill him. ROTFL here!
   - Oh Dios Mio le dijo vieja :v

In response to research question 3, we can state that, while explicit and straightforward comments on relational work are not frequent in our corpus, we do have evidence that viewers are attuned to relational work issues. We also find viewers who ask each other questions about address terms and politeness and identify (im)politeness ideologies as one of the issues among many that they are interested in when consuming Korean TV drama. As shown in Figure 5, the timed comments change the original artefact and we argue that they can contribute to making accessible the multimodal negotiations of relational work in the fictional artefacts.

6.7 Summary

In Section 6, we have illustrated the dynamic participation roles taken up by community members in the translation and negotiation of meaning of linguistically and culturally 'other' artefacts. Subtitles by community experts and comments by fans are loci of individual and collaborative processes that include translation proper as well as explicitation of cultural meaning. They illustrate the specificities of audiovisual translation, which takes place in unique multimodal contexts, and at the same time exemplify the changing roles and processes brought about by lay translation more generally.

Methodologically, combining the analysis of fansubtitles and viewer comments makes it possible to emulate more closely the fan perspective, with both types of text competing for the viewers' attention. In addition, it allows novel corpus-based approaches that can provide insights regarding translational products, but also regarding the reception and negotiation processes of the fan community.

7 Where Next?

7.1 Revisiting the Definition of Translation

This Element has taken the reader through examples of contemporary pragmatic research on different types of translation data. Some of these data types fall squarely within the purview of translation studies but have not received close linguistic attention due to the difficulty of obtaining data (such as parallel corpora of simultaneous interpreting). Other data types are different from prototypical translation, although they still can be uncontestably recognised as such (Korean series fans translating and explaining subtitles and viewers commenting on what they see). The growing interest of linguists in translation has also brought about studies on novel data types, such as people conversing with mobile phone translation apps (İkizoğlu, 2019) or translating their tasting experience into words (Mondada, forthcoming), see Section 2.

To accommodate different understandings of what counts as translation, we suggest using prototype theory borrowed from cognitive linguistics. Prototype theory is an approach to categorisation in which members of a category are not defined through a list of necessary and sufficient features, but instead in terms of overlapping sets of characteristics organised around family resemblances (Rosch, 1973). The characteristics are weighed in relation to a prototype in the centre of the category, and category members are assigned degrees of conceptual distance from the prototype and thus graded membership. In Rosch's (1978) example, a category 'bird' can be described as having salient features such as wings, light weight, ability to fly, singing or croaking, building nests, etc. According to these attributes, a robin, for instance, is a more prototypical bird, while an ostrich or a murre are more peripheral members of the bird category. The birdiness attributes are shared among these three examples in overlapping sets: ostriches and robins build nests but murres do not, murres and robins can fly but ostriches cannot, etc. This approach to categorisation has been shown to be more representative of the way humans interact with the world than traditional Aristotelian categories, since we most commonly think of a class in terms of a specific artefact or a more abstract image schema. Indeed, for many basic classes it is very difficult or impossible to provide a definition through the classic theory of concepts.

We believe that prototype theory is a useful way of thinking about what translation is as well. Written translation is commonly seen as the prototype, which is also reflected in its status as the oldest subject of analytical interest in translation studies, and the way in which subsequent research tends to describe the findings on other translation types against the backdrop of what we know about written translation. However, while most of the translation types mentioned in this Element preserve the vague commonality of 'transposition for the purpose of understanding', in some sense, hardly any specific attribute is shared by all of them. Common sets of attributes shared by the category members on the principle of family resemblance include source modality (e.g. verbal or sensual; spoken or written), target modality, the type of transposition (inter- vs. intramodal), participant constellations (one-to-one, one-to-many) or participation framework types (translator as addressee or overhearer, existence of secondary audience, involvement of human agent). The prototype approach allows us to be very inclusive and at the same time admit that some members of the category are of interest to a researcher of translation only inasmuch as they possess one or two attributes relevant to the discussion. For example, translation performed by translation apps can be studied as translation from the point of view of facilitating understanding between participants, but not in regard to the role of translator or any type of process-oriented translation research.

In this Element, we give particular weight to the attribute 'language' as it is always present, even in the more peripheral members of the category we include under the label 'translation'. For instance, the food-related sensual translation type involves language as the target medium (Gordon & Nguyen, forthcoming; Mondada, forthcoming), although, of course, it is conceivable that translation in the sense of 'facilitating understanding' might be entirely based on other semiotic systems (e.g. music translated into musical notation).

This broad, prototype-theory-inspired definition of translation as facilitating understanding between participants with language as a key attribute makes it plain that to explore all translational data types adequately, linguistic pragmatics needs to step away from the confines of a purely contrastive approach analysing two sets of linguistic and cultural practices side by side. In Section 7.2, we take stock of what interpersonal pragmatics has contributed to the study of pragmatics in translation, as reviewed in this Element.

7.2 Taking Stock

In Sections 2–4 of the Element, we surveyed the main trends in the pragmatics-oriented study of translational data. Although written translation has been treated as prototypical and has a body of research going back many decades, the interest in the mediality, participation and relational work characteristic of interpersonal pragmatics has mostly been aimed at interpreting data. This perhaps has to do with the visible presence of the interpreter as an agent in spoken contexts, whereas written translation data under-determines the who and the how of translation processes so crucial to interpersonal pragmatic analysis (although some exciting new research from the process-oriented perspective, e.g. Mees et al. (2015) on the changing roles of the written medium in the age of advanced speech recognition software, promises to influence our understanding of mediality).

Where such inroads have been made, the relational aspect of interactions between people that are affected by their understandings of culture and society has always emerged as significant. We may, for example, look back to Angermeyer's (2005a) study, which described how an interpreter's allegiance with their ethnic or national group, or with the court vs. litigants, influenced the way they chose to transform the speech of other participants. Overall, Angermeyer (2005b) concluded that features of interpersonal politeness are likely to be neglected in translation under time constraints. Later work in the interpersonal pragmatic vein shed new light on this finding (Mapson & Major, 2021) by highlighting how the translation of relational work was dependent on familiarity among conversation participants. Mapson and Major (2021) pointed out that such familiarity may actually lower cognitive load (associated with time constraints) enough to enable the interpreter to attend to relational work. Sidiropoulou (2021) drew an important distinction between the translation of fictional vs. non-fictional texts when it comes to translator-mediated reshaping of relational work. Sidiropoulou's (2021) close engagement with interpersonal pragmatics and relational work in translation brings up many important theoretical issues that we call attention to in this Element. These contributions serve as excellent illustrations of how research focusing on interpersonal pragmatics may also inform other areas that are traditionally of interest to broader translation and interpreting studies.

Research on pragmatics and audiovisual translation in recent years has shown that subtitles constitute a text genre in their own right (Guillot, 2016), formed by affordance restrictions and conventions as well as the clear desire to achieve pragmatic effects. In exploring how viewers make sense of the different multimodal inputs, the field makes strong contributions to theorising the participation structure based on discussions in telecinematic discourse studies and studies of the pragmatics of fiction. The interweaving of voices that contribute to the creation of the artefact, including products of translation processes such as subtitles and viewer comments, deserve further attention. Just as is the case with literary translation, the communicative setting of interactions between authors/collective senders, translators and recipients needs to be theorised for different reception settings and with a particular focus on aspects of interpersonal pragmatics between the different participants.

Our two case studies in Sections 5 and 6 bring to the fore typological and linguacultural differences that are worth highlighting further from a methodological and theoretical point of view. The cursory glimpse given in Section 6.2 into the manifold Korean linguistic indexicals that transfer relational meaning demonstrates that simply thinking in terms of the presence and absence of syntactic and lexical mitigation or aggravation, tallying up these strategies and assuming that the strategies might be similar in what they transfer as meaning with respect to societal ideologies cannot do justice to the complexity of the indexicals and their interplay. From this perspective, it seems that certain language translation pairs are better suited for direct comparisons than others. For instance, the pair Russian–English appears to fare better in aligning sentences and then comparing similar relational work strategies than the pair Korean–English. This is because English is more similar to Russian than to Korean both typologically and in terms of linguaculture. While this is of course no new insight, it has consequences for study design. We suggest that as a first step, a phenomenon of interest be identified (such as self-praise in Section 5 or salient negotiations of relational work in Section 6). After the unit of analysis has been identified, scholars should take stock of relational work strategies (both linguistic and – if the data permits – multimodal) in both the source and the target text that can be linked to face-enhancement, face-challenge and face-maintenance. Finally, the combined signals and their effects should be compared in the source and target texts in an attempt to bring similar and different cultural ideologies to the fore.

This survey has highlighted the areas where pragmatic research of translational data relying on the contemporary pragmatic paradigms can bring new insights into the nature of interlingual, intercultural or intermodal communication. In Section 7.3 of the Element, we propose concrete research questions that address novel data types and communicative contexts or revisit data with novel questions. We encourage researchers interested in pragmatics in translation to take up these research questions and contribute to the growing body of knowledge about facilitating understanding across languages and modes.

7.3 Future Directions in Pragmatics Research on Translation Data and Processes

In the course of our research, new ideas and research directions constantly offer themselves but cannot always be addressed for lack of time, resources or expertise. In this section, we would like to share our vision of the direction pragmatics in translation could develop in the future. The boxes below each briefly mention an issue of research, followed by potential questions and possible data sources. Although we do suggest data types associated with research questions, they should not be seen as exclusive of other translation types that exist or may appear in the course of rapid technological development. The last item in the box suggests concepts or areas of research within pragmatics that the sketched project could contribute to. The order of presentation moves from more relational work-oriented research issues, to more participation structure-oriented research, to mediality-oriented research and some more general theory-oriented research issues. These orientations can of course also be combined, as shown below.

*Projects oriented towards exploring relational work
and the participation framework*

Research issue: application of the relational work framework to written translation data and interactant/character positioning

Research question: What cues and contextual information do translators use to make appropriateness judgements or deduce illocutionary intent of the source text?

Data: aligned register-controlled corpus of written translation, e.g. CroCo (Vela & Hansen-Schirra, 2006)

Theoretical background: relational work, identity construction, text types and genres, participation framework, audience design

Research issue: application of the relational work framework to interpreting data

Research question: How do interpreters fluidly assess the appropriateness and perlocutionary effect of their output based on the addressee cues (laughter, facial expressions, unexpected second pair parts)?

Data: multimodal corpus of conference interpreting, e.g. EPTIC (Bernardini et al., 2018)

Theoretical background: relational work, text types and genres, audience design, participation framework, multimodality

Research issue: given that translators into Korean need to make relational work choices that position interactants/characters vis-à-vis each other, translators/interpreters by necessity become active shapers of interactants/characters beyond the original text

Research questions:
1. How do translators/interpreters decide on positioning?
2. Do they make different decisions depending on genre (text types, fictionality, etc.)?
3. How are different orientations towards the source and target culture juggled?

Data: comparisons of text types, interviews with translators, think-aloud recordings of translation processes

Theoretical background: relational work, identity construction, characterisation, pragmatics of fiction, language typology

Research issue: differences between professional and fan translators of fictional artefacts

Research questions:
1. Do fan translators – given their orientation to the source culture – always orient more towards foreignisation as reported in the literature, or are there exceptions that can be linked to cultural differences and difficulties/ease of accessibility of pragmatic meaning?
2. What do lay and professional translators add to the source text in light of pragmatic meaning?
3. How do lay and professional translators deal with relational work strategies?

Data: aligned corpora of professional and fan translations of different text types (e.g. manga, webtoons, comics, books, TV dramas, movies, etc.)

Theoretical background: translation strategies/orientation, participation framework, relational work, pragmatics of fiction

Research issue: in the case of subtitled telecinematic artefacts, viewers not only have the subtitles as input to arrive at interpretations of relational work, but can deduct meaning from the combined signals of the mise en scène and the spoken mode

Research question: How do viewers of subtitled telecinematic artefacts combine linguistic (source text and subtitles) and multimodal cues to arrive at interpretations of relational work?

Data: multimodally annotated corpus of scenes containing moments of relational work with source text and target text

Theoretical background: relational work, participation framework, multimodality, pragmatics of fiction

Research issue: pragmatic implications of PEMT (post-editing machine translation, i.e. using the MT to produce a raw version to be edited by a human translator), which is increasingly being used in a broad variety of situations

Research questions:
1. How successfully are interpersonal pragmatic phenomena handled in machine translation?
2. What is the contribution of the human post-editor in translating interpersonal pragmatic phenomena?

Data: aligned corpus of translation versions pre- and post-editing, accompanied by the editor's annotation, e.g. Koponen's (2016) datasets

Theoretical background: relational work strategies, post-editing

Projects oriented towards exploring participation frameworks

Research issue: participatory nature of translation in the modern world facilitated by collaborative technology

Research question: How do non-prototypical participants engage into and contribute to the translation/interpreting process?

Data: corpora of fan subtitles, creator-annotated translation memories, collections of document versions from collaborative translation environments such as Google Docs

Theoretical background: participation framework, multimodality, text types and genres, expert and lay discourses

Research issue: competence and norms in community interpreting

Research question: How do non-professional interpreters interpret within complex participation frameworks (e.g. first-person vs. third-person interpreting)?

Data: corpus of community interpreting, e.g. ComInDat (Angermeyer et al., 2013)

Theoretical background: participation framework, expert and lay discourses, high-stakes contexts

Projects oriented towards exploring participation frameworks and mediality

Research issue: growing spread of tele-interpreting instead of the presence mode

Research question: What are the consequences of the absence of contextualisation (e.g. limited visual input) for the understanding and translation of relational work in remote interpreting?

Data: corpus of aligned transcripts and recordings of remote interpreting through voice-only and videoconferencing channels

Theoretical background: participation framework, multimodality, context

Research issue: unintended production of misinformation through automated translation

Research question: Can automatic translation which is derived from limited-context negatively affect understanding through changes in illocutionary force that result from disregarding varying pragmatic norms?

Data: corpus of automatically translated social media posts (Twitter, Instagram captions and stories) and related comments

Theoretical background: relational work, automatic translation, misunderstandings, conflict

Projects oriented towards further theoretical issues in pragmatics

Research issue: ethics of translation

Research questions:
1. How do non-professional interpreters navigate varying intercultural pragmatic norms and possible negative pragmatic transfer that they might be unaware of?
2. Is there evidence of negative pragmatic transfer that non-professional interpreters might be unaware of?

Data: community interpreting in healthcare contexts, in refugee processing contexts, in disaster management contexts, e.g. datasets collected by the researchers in Balogh et al. (2021)

Theoretical background: participation framework, expert and lay discourses, high-stakes contexts

Research issue: exploring the theoretical potential of widening the scope of the definition of 'translation'

Research questions:

1. How is the concept of 'translation' fruitful when adopted in research in contexts where linguistic concerns take a backstage, such as the translation of action sequences to pictorial instructions (signs, drawings)?
2. Is it worthwhile exploring 'how-to-do-X' texts in light of how translation as knowledge on action sequences is transposed into language? What can pragmatic theorising gain from this?

Data: cooking recipes, assembly manuals, gardening instructions, etc.

Theoretical background: relational work, advisory and instruction text types/genres

As can be gleaned from the keywords and theoretical issues listed under 'theoretical background' for each potential project, two concepts highlighted in this Element (participation framework and relational work) feature prominently throughout. In addition, aspects of multimodality in the data and the aspects of mediality motivate the projects. This shows that the individual or combined perusal of the key issues introduced in this book in connection with translation data warrants further research. However, the suggested list of research issues and research questions above is far from complete and we would like to encourage scholarship in any of these areas and hope that this Element has been able to argue for some promising inroads.

References

Aijmer, K. (ed.) (2011). *Contrastive Pragmatics*. Amsterdam: John Benjamins.

Alvarez-Pereyre, M. (2011). Using film as linguistic specimen: Theoretical and practical issues. In R. Piazza, M. Bednarek & F. Rossi (eds.), *Telecinematic Discourse: Approaches to the Language of Films and Television Series*. Amsterdam: John Benjamins, pp. 47–67.

Angermeyer, P. (2005a). Who is 'I'? Pronoun choice and bilingual identity in court interpreting. *University of Pennsylvania Working Papers in Linguistics*, 11(1), 31–44.

Angermeyer, P. (2005b). Who is 'you'? Polite forms of address and ambiguous participant roles in court interpreting. *Target*, 17(2), 203–26.

Angermeyer, P., Bührig, K. & Meyer, B. (2013). Community Interpreting Database Pilot Corpus (ComInDat). Archived in Hamburger Zentrum für Sprachkorpora. Version 0.1. http://hdl.handle.net/11022/0000-0000-51E4-3

Baker, M. (1992). *In Other Words: A Coursebook on Translation*. London: Routledge.

Baker, M. (2006). Translation and context. *Journal of Pragmatics*, 38(3), 317–20.

Balogh, K., de Boe, E. & Salaets, H. (2021). Interpreter research and training: The impact of context. Special Issue of *Linguistica Antverpiensia*, 20.

Bartłomiejczyk, M. (2016). *Face Threats in Interpreting: A Pragmatic Study of Plenary Debates in the European Parliament*. Katowice: Wydawnictwo Uniwersytetu Śląskiego.

Bartłomiejczyk, M. (2020). Parliamentary impoliteness and the interpreter's gender. *Pragmatics*, 30(4), 459–84.

Bassnett, S. (2012). The translator as cross-cultural mediator. In K. Malmkjær & Kevin Windle (eds.), *The Oxford Handbook of Translation Studies*. Oxford: Oxford University Press, pp. 1–9.

Baumgarten, N. (2017). Pragmatics and translation. In A. Baron, Y. Gu & G. Steen (eds.), *The Routledge Handbook of Pragmatics*. London: Routledge, pp. 521–34.

Bednarek, M. A. (2011). *The Stability of the Televisual Character: A Corpus Stylistic Case Study*. Amsterdam: John Benjamins.

Bell, A. (1984). Language style as audience design. *Language in Society*, 13(2), 145–204.

Bendazzoli, C., & Sandrelli, A. (2005). An approach to corpus-based interpreting studies: Developing EPIC (European Parliament Interpreting Corpus). In H. Gerzymisch-Arbogast & S. Nauert (eds.), *MuTra 2005 – Challenges of*

Multidimensional Translation, pp. 1–12. www.euroconferences.info/proceed ings/2005_Proceedings/2005_Bendazzoli_Sandrelli.pdf.

Bendazzoli, C. & Sandrelli, A. (2009). Corpus-based interpreting studies: Early work and future prospects. *Revista Tradumatica*, 7, 1–9.

Berk-Seligson, S. (1988). The impact of politeness in witness testimony: The influence of the court interpreter. *Multilingua*, 7(4), 411–40.

Bernardini, S., Ferraresi, A., Russo, M., Collard, C. & Defrancq, B. (2018). Building interpreting and intermodal corpora: A how-to for a formidable task. In M. Russo, C. Bendazzoli & B. Defrancq (eds.), *Making Way in Corpus-Based Interpreting Studies*. Singapore: Springer Nature, pp. 21–42.

Biagini, M., Sandrelli, A. & Davitti, E. (2017). Participation in interpreter-mediated interaction: Shifting along a multidimensional continuum [Special Issue]. *Journal of Pragmatics*, 107.

Blum-Kulka, S. (1981). The study of translation in view of new developments in discourse analysis: The problem of indirect speech acts. *Poetics Today*, 2 (4), 89–95.

Blum-Kulka, S. & Olshtain, E. (1984). Requests and apologies: A cross-cultural study of speech act realization patterns. *Applied Linguistics*, 5(3), 196–213.

Bonsignori, V. & Bruti, S. (2015). Conversational routines across languages: The case of greetings and leave-takings in original and dubbed films. In J. Díaz Cintas & J. Neves (eds.), *Audiovisual Translation: Taking Stock*. Newcastle upon Tyne: Cambridge Scholar Publishing, pp. 28–45.

Bonsignori, V., Bruti, S. & Masi, S. (2011). Formulae across languages: English greetings, leave-takings and good wishes in dubbed Italian. In J.-M. Lavaur, A. Matamala & A. Serban (eds.), *Audiovisual Translation in Close-Up: Practical and Theoretical Approaches*. Bern: Peter Lang, pp. 23–44.

Bonsignori, V., Bruti, S. & Masi, S. (2012). Exploring greetings and leave-takings in original and dubbed language. In A. Remael, P. Orero & M. Carroll (eds.), *Audiovisual Translation and Media Accessibility at the Crossroads: Media for All 3*. Amsterdam: Rodopi, pp. 357–79.

Brock, A. (2015). Participation frameworks and participation in televised sitcom, candid camera and stand-up comedy. In M. Dynel & J. Chovanec (eds.), *Participation in Public and Social Media Interactions*. Amsterdam: John Benjamins, pp. 27–47.

Brown, L. (2011). *Korean Honorifics and Politeness in Second Language Learning*. Amsterdam: John Benjamins.

Brown, L. (2015). Honorifics and politeness. In L. Brown & J. Yeon (eds.), *The Handbook of Korean Linguistics*. Chichester: Wiley Blackwell, pp. 303–19.

Brown, L. & Winter, B. (2019). Multimodal indexicality in Korean: "Doing deference" and "performing intimacy" through nonverbal behavior. *Journal of Politeness Research*, 15(1), 25–54.

Brown, P. & Levinson, S. (1987). *Politeness: Some Universals in Language Usage*. Cambridge: Cambridge University Press.

Bruti, S. (2006). Cross-cultural pragmatics: The translation of implicit compliments in subtitles. *The Journal of Specialised Translation*, 6(1), 185–97.

Bruti, S. (2007). Translating compliments and insults in the Pavia Corpus of Film Dialogue: Two sides of the same coin? In M. Freddi & M. Pavesi (eds.), *Analysing Audiovisual Dialogue: Linguistic and Translational Insights*. Bologna: Clueb, pp. 143–63.

Bruti, S. (2009). The translation of compliments in subtitles. In J. Díaz Cintas (ed.), *New Trends in Audiovisual Translation*. Bristol: Multilingual Matters, pp. 226–38.

Bubel, C. M. (2006). The linguistic construction of character relations in TV drama: Doing friendship in *Sex and the City*. PhD dissertation. Saarbrücken: Saarland University.

Bubel, C. M. (2008). Film audiences as overhearers. *Journal of Pragmatics*, 40 (1), 55–71.

Chafe, W. (1980). The deployment of consciousness in the construction of narrative. In W. Chafe (ed.), *The Pear Stories: Cognitive, Cultural and Linguistic Aspects of Narrative Production*. Norwood, NJ: Ablex, pp. 9–50.

Chang, C.-C. & Wu, M. M. (2009). Address form shifts in interpreted Q&A sessions. *Interpreting*, 11(2), 164–89.

Chesterman, A., Dam, H. V., Engberg, J. & Schjoldager, A. (2003). Bananas: On names and definitions in translation studies. *Hermes*, 16(31), 197–209.

Cheung, A. (2012). The use of reported speech by court interpreters in Hong Kong. *Interpreting*, 14(1), 73–91.

Cheung, A. (2014). The use of reported speech and the perceived neutrality of court interpreters. *Interpreting*, 16(2), 191–208.

Choo, M. (2006). The structure and use of Korean honorifics. In H.-m. Sohn (ed.), *Korean Language in Culture and Society*. Manoa: University of Hawai'i Press, pp. 132–45.

Clark, H. H. (1996). *Using Language*. Cambridge: Cambridge University Press.

Colvin, C. R., Block, J. & Funder, D. (1995). Overly positive self-evaluations and personality: Negative implications for mental health. *Journal of Personality and Social Psychology*, 68(6), 1152–62.

Cooren, F. (2004). Textual agency: How texts do things in organizational settings. *Organization*, 11(3), 373–93.

Cooren, F. (2008). Between semiotics and pragmatics: Opening language studies to textual agency. *Journal of Pragmatics*, 40(1), 1–16.

Coupland, J. (1996). Dating advertisements: Discourses of the commodified self. *Discourse & Society*, 7(2), 187–207.

Culpeper, J. (1996). Towards an anatomy of impoliteness. *Journal of Pragmatics*, 25(2), 349–67.

Dayter, D. (2016). *Discursive Self in Microblogging: Speech Acts, Stories and Self-Praise*. Amsterdam: John Benjamins.

Dayter, D. (2021a). Strategies in a corpus of simultaneous interpreting. Effects of directionality, phraseological complexity, and position in speech event. *Meta: Translator's Journal*, 66(3), 594–617.

Dayter, D. (2021b). Dealing with interactionally risky speech acts in simultaneous interpreting: The case of self-praise. *Journal of Pragmatics*, 174, 28–42.

Defrancq, B. (2015). Corpus-based research into the presumed effects of short EVS. *Interpreting*, 17(1), 26–45.

Desilla, L. (2019). Pragmatics and audiovisual translation. In L. Pérez-González (ed.), *The Routledge Handbook of Audiovisual Translation*. London: Routledge, pp. 242–59.

Díaz Cintas, J. & Muñoz Sánchez, P. (2006). Fansubs: Audiovisual translation in an amateur environment. *The Journal of Specialised Translation*, 6(6), 37–52.

Dynel, M. (2011). 'You talking to me?' The viewer as a ratified listener to film discourse. *Journal of Pragmatics*, 43(6), 1628–44.

Eelen, G. (2001). *A Critique of Politeness Theories*. Manchester: St. Jerome Publishing.

Friedrich, P. (1989). Language, ideology, and political economy. *American Anthropologist*, 91(2), 295–312.

Fauconnier, G. (1985). *Mental Spaces: Aspects of Meaning Construction in Natural Language*. Cambridge: Cambridge University Press.

Gallai, F. (2019) Cognitive pragmatics and translation studies. In R. Tipton & L. Desilla (eds.), *The Routledge Handbook of Translation and Pragmatics*. London: Routledge, pp. 51–72.

Gartzonika, O. & Serban, A. (2009). Greek soldiers on the screen: Politeness, fluency and audience design in subtitling. In J. Díaz Cintas (ed.), *New Trends in Audiovisual Translation*. London: Multilingual Matters, pp. 239–50.

Genette, G. (1997). *Paratexts: Thresholds of Interpretation*. Cambridge: Cambridge University Press.

Gibb, R. & Good, A. (2014). Interpretation, translation and intercultural communication in refugee status determination procedures in the UK and France. *Language and Intercultural Communication*, 14(3), 385–99.

Glémet, R. (1958). Conference interpreting. In A. H. Smith (ed.), *Aspects of Translation*. London: Secker and Warburg, pp. 105–22.

Goffman, E. (1981). *Forms of Talk*. Philadelphia: University of Pennsylvania Press.

Golato, A. (2005). *Compliments and Compliment Responses. Grammatical Structure and Sequential Organization*. Amsterdam: Benjamins.

Gordon, C. & Nguyen, M. (forthcoming). Chef Knows Best: How "Translations" of an Immigrant Family's Recipes (Re)construct a Celebrity Chef's Epistemic Authority. In M. Locher, D. Dayter & T. Messerli (eds.), *Pragmatics in Translation*. Amsterdam: Benjamins.

Gottlieb, H. (1994). Subtitling: Diagonal translation. *Perspectives*, 2(1), 101–21.

Graën, J. (2018). Exploiting alignment in multiparallel corpora for applications in linguistics and language learning. Unpublished PhD dissertation, University of Zurich, Faculty of Arts.

Guillot, M.-N. (2010). Film subtitles from a cross-cultural pragmatics perspective: Issues of linguistic and cultural representation. *Translator*, 16(1), 67–92.

Guillot, M.-N. (2016). Cross-cultural pragmatics and audiovisual translation. *Target*, 28(2), 288–301.

Guillot, M.-N. (2017). Subtitling and dubbing in telecinematic text. In M. A. Locher & A. H. Jucker (eds.), *Handbooks of Pragmatics: Pragmatics of Fiction*. Berlin: Mouton de Gruyter, pp. 397–424.

Guillot, M.-N. (2020). The pragmatics of audiovisual translation: Voices from within in film subtitling. *Journal of Pragmatics*, 170, 317–30.

Gutt, E.-A. (1998). Pragmatic aspects of translation. Some relevance-theory observations. In L. Hickey (ed.), *The Pragmatics of Translation*. Clevedon: Multilingual Matters, pp.41–53.

Hatim, B. (1998). Text politeness: A semiotic regime for a more interactive pragmatics. In L. Hickey (ed.), *The Pragmatics of Translation*. Clevedon: Multilingual Matters, pp. 72–102.

Hatim, B. & Mason, I. (1997). *The Translator as Communicator*. London: Routledge.

Hatim, B. & Mason, I. (2000). Politeness in screen translation. In L. Venuti (ed.), *The Translation Studies Reader*. London: Routledge, pp. 430–45.

Hickey, L. ed. (1998). *The Pragmatics of Translation*. Clevedon: Multilingual Matters.

Holmes, J. S. ([1972] 2000). The name and nature of translation studies. In L. Venuti (ed.), *The Translation Studies Reader*. London: Routledge, pp. 172–85.

House, J. (1977). *A Model for Translation Quality Assessment*. Tübingen: Narr.

House, J. (2006). Text and context in translation. *Journal of Pragmatics*, 38(3), 338–58.

House, J. (2015). *Translation as Communication across Languages and Cultures*. London: Routledge.

House, J. (2018a). Translation studies and pragmatics. In C. Ilie & N. R. Norrick (eds.), *Pragmatics and its Interfaces*. Amsterdam: John Benjamins, pp. 143–62.

House, J. (2018b). *Translation: The Basics*. London: Routledge.

House, J. & Kádár, D. Z. (2021). *Cross-Cultural Pragmatics*. Cambridge: Cambridge University Press.

Hymes, D. (1964). Introduction: Toward ethnographies of communication. *American Anthropologist*, 66(6), 1–34.

Hymes, Dell. 1972. Models of the interaction of language and social life. In J. Gumperz & D. Hymes (eds.), *Directions in Sociolinguistics: The Ethnography of Communication*. New York: Holt, Rinehart and Winston, Inc., pp. 35–71.

İkizoğlu, D. (2019). "What did it say?": Mobile phone translation app as participant and object in family discourse. *Journal of Pragmatics*, 147, 1–16.

Jacobsen, B. (2008). Interactional pragmatics and court interpreting: An analysis of face. *Interpreting*, 10(1), 128–58.

Jäger, G. (1975). *Translation und Translationslinguistik*. Halle Saale: Niemeyer.

Kade, O. (1968). *Zufall und Gesetzmäßigkeit in der Übersetzung*. Leipzig: Enzyklopädie.

Kecskes, I. (2013). *Intercultural Pragmatics*. Oxford: Oxford University Press.

Kefala, S. (2021). The pragmatics of translated tourism advertising. *Journal of Pragmatics*, 173, 88–100.

Keselman, O., Cederborg, A.-C. & Linell, P. (2010). "That is not necessary for you to know!": Negotiation of participation status of unaccompanied children in interpreter-mediated asylum hearings. *Interpreting*, 12(1), 83–104.

Kiaer, J. (2018). *The Routledge Course in Korean Translation*. London: Routledge.

King, R. (2006). Korean kinship terminology. In H.-m. Sohn (ed.), *Korean Language in Culture and Society*. Manoa: University of Hawai'i Press, pp. 101–17.

Knapp-Potthoff, A. & Knapp, K. (1987). The man (or woman) in the middle: Discoursal aspects of non-professional interpreting. In K. Knapp, W. Enninger & A. Knapp-Potthoff (eds.), *Analyzing Intercultural Communication*. Berlin: Mouton de Gruyter, pp. 181–211.

Koh, H. E. (2006). Usage of Korean address and reference terms. In H.-m. Sohn (ed.), *Korean Language in Culture and Society*. Manoa: University of Hawai'i Press, pp. 146–54.

Koponen, M. (2016). Machine translation post-editing and effort. Empirical studies on the post-editing process. Unpublished PhD dissertation, University of Helsinki, Faculty of Arts. https://helda.helsinki.fi/bitstream/handle/10138/160256/machinet.pdf.

Kruger, H. & van Rooy, B. (2016). Constrained language. *English World-Wide*, 37(1), 26–57.

Kuijpers, M. M. (2021). Exploring the dimensional relationships of story world absorption: A commentary on the role of attention during absorbed reading. *Scientific Study of Literature*, 11(2), 266–82.

Kurz, I. & Pöchhacker, F. (1995). Quality in TV interpreting. *Translatio. Nouvelles de la FIT— FIT Newsletter*, 14(3/4), 350–8.

Lakoff, R. (1973). The logic of politeness, or minding your p's and q's. *Chicago Linguistics Society*, 9, 292–305.

Lee, J. (2013). A study of facework in interpreter-mediated courtroom examination. *Perspectives: Studies in Translatology*, 21(1), 82–99.

Leech, G. (1983). *Principles of Pragmatics*. London: Longman.

Levinson, S. (2004). Deixis. In L. Horn & G. Ward (eds.), *The Handbook of Pragmatics*. Oxford: Blackwell, pp. 97–121.

Licoppe, C. & Veyrier, C.-A. (2017). How to show the interpreter on screen? The normative organization of visual ecologies in multilingual courtrooms with video links. *Journal of Pragmatics*, 107, 147–64.

Linguistic Politeness Research Group (eds.). (2011). *Discursive Approaches to Politeness*. Berlin: de Gruyter Mouton.

Locher, M. A. (2006). Polite behavior within relational work: The discursive approach to politeness. *Multilingua: Journal of Cross-Cultural and Interlanguage Communication*, 25(3), 249–67.

Locher, M. A. (2008). Relational work, politeness and identity construction. In G. Antos, E. Ventola & T. Weber (eds.), *Handbooks of Applied Linguistics. Volume 2: Interpersonal Communication*. Berlin: Mouton de Gruyter, pp. 509–40.

Locher, M. A. (2017). Multilingualism in fiction. In M. A. Locher & A. H. Jucker (eds.), *Pragmatics of Fiction*. Berlin: de Gruyter Mouton, pp. 297–327.

Locher, M. A. (2020). Moments of relational work in English fan translations of Korean TV drama. *Journal of Pragmatics*, 170, 139–55.

Locher, M. A. & Graham, S. L. (eds.) (2010). *Interpersonal Pragmatics* (Vol. 6). Berlin: Mouton.

Locher, M. A. & Jucker, A. H. (eds.) (2017). *Pragmatics of Fiction*. Berlin: de Gruyter Mouton.

Locher, M. A. & Jucker, A. H. (2021). *The Pragmatics of Fiction. Literature, Stage and Screen Discourse*. Edinburgh: Edinburgh University Press.

Locher, M. A., Jucker, A. H., Landert, D., & Messerli, T. C. (2023). *Fiction and Pragmatics*. Cambridge: Cambridge University Press.

Locher, M. A. & Messerli, T. C. (2020). Translating the other: Communal TV watching of Korean TV drama. *Journal of Pragmatics*, 170, 20–36.

Locher, M. A. & Messerli, T. C. (forthcoming). "what does hyung mean please?" Moments of teaching and learning about Korean im/politeness on an online streaming platform of Korean TV drama. In M. Shin Kim (ed.), *Politeness in Korean*. Springer.

Locher, M. A. & Sidiropoulou, M. (2021). Introducing the special issue on the pragmatics of translation. *Journal of Pragmatics*, 178, 121–6.

Locher, M. A. & Watts, R. J. (2005). Politeness theory and relational work. *Journal of Politeness Research*, 1(1), 9–33.

Locher, M. A. & Watts, R. J. (2008). Relational work and impoliteness: Negotiating norms of linguistic behaviour. In D. Bousfield & M. A. Locher (eds.), *Impoliteness in Language. Studies on its Interplay with Power in Theory and Practice*. Berlin: Mouton de Gruyter, pp. 77–99.

Magnifico, C. & Defrancq, B. (2017). Hedges in conference interpreting. *Interpreting*, 19(1), 21–46.

Malmkjaer, K. (1998). Cooperation and literary translation. In L. Hickey (ed.), *The Pragmatics of Translation*. Clevedon: Multilingual Matters, pp. 25–40.

Manes, J. & Wolfson, N. (1981). The compliment formula. In C. Florian (ed.), *Conversational Routine. Explorations in Standardized Communication Situations and Prepatterned Speech*. The Hague: Mouton, pp. 115–32.

Mapson, R. (2015). Interpreting linguistic politeness from British Sign Language to English. PhD dissertation. Bristol: University of Bristol.

Mapson, R. & Major, G. (2021). Interpreters, rapport, and the role of familiarity. *Journal of Pragmatics*, 176, 63–75.

Mason, I. (2000). Audience design in translating. *The Translator*, 6(1), 1–22.

Mason, I. & Stewart, M. (2001). Interactional pragmatics, face and the dialogue interpreter. In I. Mason (ed.), *Triadic Exchanges. Studies in Dialogue Interpre*ting. Manchester: St. Jerome, pp.51–70.

Massidda, S. (2015). *Audiovisual Translation in the Digital Age: The Italian Fansubbing Phenomenon*. Basingstoke: Palgrave Macmillan.

Matley, D. (2017). "This is NOT a #humblebrag, this is just a #brag": The pragmatics of self-praise, hashtags and politeness in Instagram posts. *Discourse, Context and Media* 22, 30–8.

Mees, I. M., Dragsted, B., Gorm Hansen, I. & Jakobsen, A. L. (2015). Sound effects in translation. In M. Ehrensberger-Dow, S. Göpferich & S. O'Brien (eds.), *Interdisciplinarity in Translation and Interpreting Process Research*. Amsterdam: John Benjamins, pp. 141–55.

Messerli, T. C. (2017). Participation structure in fictional discourse: Authors, scriptwriters, audiences and characters. In M. A. Locher & A. H. Jucker (eds.), *Pragmatics of Fiction. Handbooks of Pragmatics* (Vol. 12). Berlin: Mouton de Gruyter, pp. 25–54.

Messerli, T. C. (2019). Subtitles and cinematic meaning-making: Interlingual subtitles as textual agents. *Multilingua*, 38(5), 529–46.

Messerli, T. C. (2020). Subtitled artefacts as communication: The case of *Ocean's Eleven* scene 12. *Perspectives*, 28(6), 851–63.

Messerli, T. (2021). *Repetition in Telecinematic Humour: How US American Sitcoms Employ Formal and Semantic Repetition in the Construction of Multimodal Humour.* Freiburg: NIHIN.

Messerli, T. C. & Locher, M. A. (2021). Humour support and emotive stance in comments on K-Drama. *Journal of Pragmatics*, 178, 408–25.

Meyer, B. (2008). Interpreting proper names: Different interventions in simultaneous and consecutive interpreting? *trans-kom*, 1(1), 105–22.

Meyer, B. (2010). Consecutive and simultaneous interpreting (CoSi). Archived in Hamburger Zentrum für Sprachkorpora. Version 1.1. http://hdl.handle.net/11022/0000-0000-5225-A.

Miskovic-Lukovic, M. & Dedaic, M. N. (2012). The discourse marker odnosno at the ICTY: A case of disputed translation in war crime trials. *Journal of Pragmatics*, 44(10), 1355–77.

Mondada, L. (forthcoming). From the sensing body to language, and back: Tasting and expressing taste. In M. A. Locher, T. C. Messerli & D. Dayter (eds.), *Pragmatics and Translation.* Amsterdam: John Benjamins.

Moore, J. (2013). *Do Your Best and Trust God for the Rest.* Nashville, TN: Abingdon Press.

Morini, M. (2013). *The Pragmatic Translator: An Integral Theory of Translation.* London: Bloomsbury.

Morini, M. (2019) "The relations of signs to interpreters": Translating readers and characters from English to Italian. In R. Tipton & L. Desilla (eds.), *The Routledge Handbook of Translation and Pragmatics.* London: Routledge, pp. 193–205.

Moser-Mercer, B. (2000). Simultaneous interpreting: Cognitive potential and limitations. *Interpreting*, 5(2), 83–94.

Mubenga, K. S. (2009). Towards a multimodal pragmatic analysis of film discourse in audiovisual translation. *Meta: Journal Des Traducteurs*, 54(3), 466–84.

Nakane, I. (2014). *Interpreter-Mediated Police Interviews.* London: Palgrave Macmillan.

Napoli, V. (2021). *Requests in Film Dialogue and Dubbing Translation. A Comparative Study of English and Italian.* Cambridge: Cambridge Scholars Publishing.

Neubert, A. (1968). Pragmatische Aspekte der Übersetzung. In A. Neubert (ed.), *Grundfragen der Übersetzungswissenschaft.* Leipzig: Karl-Marx-Universität Leipzig, pp. 21–33.

Nida, E. (1964) *Towards a Science of Translation.* Leiden: Brill.

Oksefjell-Ebeling, S. (2012). Textual reduction in translated dialogue in film versus literary fiction. *Nordic Journal of English Studies*, 11(3), 100–26.

Pablos-Ortega, C. (2019). "I'm so sorry to disturb you, but I wonder if I could have your autograph" versus ¿Me firma un autógrafo por favor?: Contrastive (in) directness in subtitling. In R. Tipton & L. Desilla (eds.), *The Routledge Handbook of Translation and Pragmatics.* London: Routledge, pp. 205–24.

Papacharissi, Z. (2015). Affective publics and structures of storytelling: Sentiment, events and mediality. *Information, Communication & Society*, 19(3), 307–24.

Pavesi, M. & Formentelli, M. (2019). Comparing insults across languages in films: Dubbing as cross-cultural mediation. *Multilingua*, 38(5), 563–82.

Pérez-González, L. (2019). Rewriting the circuitry of audiovisual translation. In L. Pérez-González (ed.), *The Routledge Handbook of Audiovisual Translation.* London: Routledge, pp. 1–12.

Pettit, Z. (2009). Connecting cultures: Cultural transfer in subtitling and dubbing. In J. Díaz Cintas (ed.), *New Trends in Audiovisual Translation.* Bristol: Multilingual Matters, pp. 44–57.

Planchenault, G. (2017). Doing dialects in dialogues: Regional, social and ethnic variation in fiction. In M. A. Locher & A. H. Jucker (eds.), *Pragmatics of Fiction.* Berlin: de Gruyter Mouton, pp. 265–96.

Pöchhacker, F. (2004). *Introducing Interpreting Studies.* London: Routledge.

Pöllabauer, S. (2007). Interpreting in asylum hearings: Issues of saving face. In C. Wadensjö, B. Englund-Dimitrova & A. L. Nilsson (eds.), *The Critical Link 4. Professionalisation of Interpreting in the Community.* Amsterdam: John Benjamins, pp. 39–52.

Pollali, C.-S. & Sidiropoulou, M. (2021). Identity formation and patriarchal voices in theatre translation. *Journal of Pragmatics*, 177, 97–108.

Pomerantz, A. (1980). Telling my side: "Limited access" as a fishing device. *Sociological Inquiry*, 50(3–4), 186–98.

Ramos Pinto, S. (2018). Film, dialects and subtitles: An analytical framework for the study of non-standard varieties in subtitling. *The Translator*, 24(1), 17–34.

Remael, A. (2010). Audiovisual translation. In Y. Gambier & L. van Doorslaer (eds.), *Handbook of Translation Studies*. Amsterdam: John Benjamins, pp. 12–17.

Rhee, S. & Koo, H. J. (2017). Audience-blind sentence-enders in Korean: A discourse-pragmatic perspective. *Journal of Pragmatics*, 120, 101–21.

Rosch, E. (1973). Natural categories. *Cognitive Psychology*, 4(3), 328–50.

Rosch, E. (1978). *Principles of Categorization*. In E. Rosch & B. Lloyd (eds.), *Cognition and Categorization*. Hillsdale, NJ: Lawrence Elbaum Associates, pp. 28–49.

Rüdiger, S. & Dayter. D. (2020). Manbragging online: Self-praise on pick-up artists' forums. *Journal of Pragmatics*, 161, 16–27.

Russo, M., Bendazzoli, C., Sandrelli, A. & Spinolo, N. (2012). The European Parliament Interpreting Corpus (EPIC): Implementation and developments. In F. Straniero Sergio & C. Falbo (eds.), *Breaking Ground in Corpus-Based Interpreting Studies*. Bern: Peter Lang, pp. 53–90.

Savvalidou, F. (2011). Interpreting (im)politeness strategies in a media political setting: A case study from the Greek prime ministerial TV debate as interpreted into Greek Sign Language. In L. Leeson, S. Wurm & M. Vermeerbergen (eds.), *Signed Language Interpreting: Preparation, Practice and Performance*. Manchester: St. Jerome, pp. 87–109.

Setton, R. (2003). Models of interpreting process. In A. Collados Ais & J. A. Sabio Pinilla (eds.), *Avances en la investigación sobre interpretación*. Granada: Comares, pp. 29–89.

Setton, R. (2006). Context in simultaneous interpretation. *Journal of Pragmatics*, 38(3), 374–89.

Sidiropoulou, M. (2020). Understanding migration through translating the multimodal code. *Journal of Pragmatics*, 170, 284–300.

Sidiropoulou, M. (2021). *Understanding Im/politeness through Translation. The English-Greek Paradigm*. Cham: Springer Nature Switzerland.

Speer, S. (2012). The interactional organization of self-praise: Epistemics, preference organization, and implications for identity research. *Social Psychology Quarterly*, 75(1), 52–79.

Spencer-Oatey, H. (2000). Rapport management: A framework for analysis. In H. Spencer-Oatey (ed.), *Culturally Speaking: Managing Rapport through Talk across Cultures*. London: Continuum, pp. 11–46.

Spencer-Oatey, H. (2005a) Rapport management theory and culture. *Interactional Pragmatics*, 2(3), 335–46.

Spencer-Oatey, H. (2005b). (Im)Politeness, face and perceptions of rapport: Unpackaging their bases and interrelationships. *Journal of Politeness Research*, 1(1), 95–119.

Spencer-Oatey, H. & Franklin, P. (2009) *Intercultural Interaction. A Multidisciplinary Perspective on Intercultural Communication*. Basingstoke: Palgrave MacMillan.

Sperber, D. & Wilson, D. (1995). *Relevance: Communication and Cognition* (Second ed.). Oxford: Blackwell.

Ticca, A. C. & Traverso, V. (2017). Participation in bilingual interactions: Translating, interpreting and mediating documents in a French social centre. *Journal of Pragmatics*, 107, 129–46.

Tipton, R. & Desilla, L. (eds.) (2019). *The Routledge Handbook of Translation and Pragmatics*. London: Routledge.

Tomaszkiewicz, T. (1993). *Les opérations linguistiques qui sous-tendent le processus de sous-titrage des films*. Poznan: Adam Mickiewicz University Press.

Toury, G. (1995). *Descriptive Translation Studies and Beyond*. Amsterdam: John Benjamins.

Underwood, K. (2011). Facework as self-heroicisation: A case study of three elderly women. *Journal of Pragmatics*, 43(8), 2215–42.

Van de Mieroop, D. (2012). The quotative 'he/she says' in interpreted doctor–patient interaction. *Interpreting*, 14(1), 92–117.

Van Dijk, T. A. (2001). Discourse, ideology and context. *Folia Linguistica*, 35(1–2), 11–40.

Varela, F. C. (2002). Models of research in audiovisual translation. *Babel*, 48(1), 1–13.

Vela, M. & Hansen-Schirra, S. (2006). The use of multi-level annotation and alignment for the translator. In *Proceedings of the ASLIB Translating and the Computer 28 conference*, London, 16–17 November. http://fedora.clarin-d.uni-saarland.de/croco-gecco/croco/vela_hansenschirra_aslib2006.pdf.

Wadensjö, C. (1998). *Interpreting as Interaction*. London: Longman.

Wadensjö, C. (2008). In and off the Show: Co-constructing 'invisibility' in an interpreter-mediated talk show interview. *Meta: Translators' Journal*, 53(1), 184–203.

Watts, R. (2005). Linguistic politeness research. Quo vadis? In R. Watts, S. Ide & K. Ehlich (eds.), *Politeness in Language: Studies in its History, Theory and Practice*. Berlin: Mouton de Gruyter, pp. xi–xlvii.

Wu, R. (2011). A conversation analysis of self-praising in everyday Mandarin interaction. *Journal of Pragmatics*, 43(13), 3152–76.

Yuh, Leighanne Kimberly. (2020). *From Aristocrats to Slaves: An Examination of Social Stratification from Traditional to Modern Times in Korea*. The Australia Centre, The Australian Embassy: Seoul, South Korea.

Zhan, C. (2012). Mediation through personal pronoun shifts in dialogue interpreting of political meetings. *Interpreting*, 14(2), 192–216.

Acknowledgements

We thank the anonymous reviewers and general editors for their constructive feedback, which helped to strengthen our line of argumentation. This open access manuscript has been published with the support of the Swiss National Science Foundation.

Funding Statement

Published with the support of the Swiss National Science Foundation.

Cambridge Elements ≡

Pragmatics

Jonathan Culpeper

Lancaster University, UK

Jonathan Culpeper is Professor of English Language and Linguistics in the Department of Linguistics and English Language at Lancaster University, UK. A former co-editor-in-chief of the *Journal of Pragmatics* (2009–14), with research spanning multiple areas within pragmatics, his major publications include: *Impoliteness: Using Language to Cause Offence* (2011, CUP) and *Pragmatics and the English Language* (2014, Palgrave; with Michael Haugh).

Michael Haugh

University of Queensland, Australia

Michael Haugh is Professor of Linguistics and Applied Linguistics in the School of Languages and Cultures at the University of Queensland, Australia. A former co-editor-in-chief of the *Journal of Pragmatics* (2015–2020), with research spanning multiple areas within pragmatics, his major publications include: *Understanding Politeness* (2013, CUP; with Dániel Kádár), *Pragmatics and the English Language* (2014, Palgrave; with Jonathan Culpeper), and *Im/politeness Implicatures* (2015, Mouton de Gruyter).

Advisory Board

About the Series

Cambridge Elements in Pragmatics showcases dynamic and high-quality original, concise and accessible scholarly works. Written for a broad pragmatics readership, it encourages dialogue across different perspectives on language use. It is a forum for cutting-edge work in pragmatics: consolidating theory, leading the development of new methods, and advancing innovative topics in the field.

Cambridge Elements ≡

Pragmatics

Elements in the Series

Advice in Conversation
Nele Põldvere, Rachele De Felice and Carita Paradis

Positive Social Acts: The Brighter and Darker Sides of Sociability
Roni Danziger

Pragmatics in Translation: Mediality, Participation and Relational Work
Daria Dayter, Miriam A. Locher and Thomas C. Messerli

Fiction and Pragmatics
Miriam A. Locher, Andreas H. Jucker, Daniela Landert and Thomas C. Messerli

A full series listing is available at: www.cambridge.org/EIPR

Printed in the United States
by Baker & Taylor Publisher Services